Analytic Theology

A Bibliography

Analytic Theology

A Bibliography

William J. Abraham

Highland Loch Press
Dallas, Texas, USA

In association with
Wordsmith Academic Press

To
J. R. Lucas

Acknowledgements

I am delighted to acknowledge the help of Mark Wiebe, David Mahfood, Dr. Heather Oglevie, and Anthony Cunningham in the preparation of this bibliography.

Contents

Introduction

This bibliography is a work in progress. It is intended to gather together material cultivated within analytic philosophy on the various loci of systematic theology. Ideally it constitutes a beginning bibliography in analytic theology. In my judgment the time is ripe for the development of such a bibliography. Over the last generation we have seen an extraordinary revival of first rate work in the philosophy of religion and in philosophical theology. Regrettably the truth of this claim is often overlooked in reviews of current work in philosophy. Taken as a whole this material covers a wide range of topics that pick up conceptual and epistemological issues in religion. It is striking how much of this material is now devoted to philosophical reflection on Christian doctrine. This in turn leads directly into doing work in theology proper, that is, articulating normative claims about the most appropriate content of Christian teaching for today. It is this latter development that prompts the move to look at the role of analytic philosophy within systematic theology and to designate this work as "analytic theology". One way to think about analytic theology is to think of it precisely as systematic theology done in such a way that it draws intentionally and systematically on the skills and resources of analytic philosophy. I argue the case for this in the introductory essay, "Systematic theology as Analytic Theology", which is reprinted here by permission of Oxford University Press.[1]

---

[1] It was originally published in a volume edited by Oliver D. Crisp and Michael C. Rea, *Analytic Theology: New Essays in the*

The bibliography does not confine itself to work done by theologians and philosophers trained in the analytic tradition. It is also includes other historical and systematic material that should prove useful to those interested in analytic theology. Choices at this level very much reflect my own initial reflections. I hope that future editions will be more representative. Ideally we really need a robust bibliography that will provide both theological and philosophical material relevant to the development of analytic theology. Such a collection would enable philosophers get their initial bearings within theology and help theologians get their initial bearings within analytic philosophy. Here the weight falls on the provision of philosophical material for theologians.

It is important at the outset to identify one version of the classical loci of systematic theology used in organizing the material. The following list provides the sequence roughly but not slavishly followed in traditional volumes of Christian theology. Prolegomenon: task, sources, norms, method, scripture; God: the existence of God, attributes, Trinity (three persons in one substance or essence), (economic Trinity and immanent Trinity); Creation: creature (world, human beings), providence (law, miracle, evil), the human condition (the image of God, sin); Christology: the person of Jesus Christ (two natures in one person) the work of Jesus Christ (prophet – revelation, priest – reconciliation, king - deliverance, atonement); Pneumatology: the person and work of the Holy Spirit; Ecclesiology: the nature of the Church, Word and sacraments, ministry, purpose or mission; Soteriology: salvation, justification, sanctification, theosis; Eschatology (the Last Things): death and eternal

Philosophy of Theology (Oxford: Oxford University Press, 2009), 54-69.

life (personal eschatology: death, the intermediate state, heaven, hell, and ultimate destiny), (cosmic eschatology: parousia or return of Christ, the final destiny of all things). This bibliography operates with a version of this sequence of topics in systematic theology. There has been much debate about the origins of this network of topics. Some have tracked it to developments in medieval theology in early scholasticism. In my view these topics arise from the issues picked up in the early creeds of the Church; and these topics in turn were determined by intellectual, pastoral, and soteriological concerns clearly visible in the evangelization of the Roman Empire. Whatever their origin it is obvious that analytic theology, if it is at all to be taken seriously as theology, must ultimately deal with the whole gamut of topics that are of concern to theology. It is not enough simply to cherry pick this or that topic and run with it philosophically, for in both theology and philosophy the topics which have to be explored have systematic interrelationships. What one proposes on one topic has implications for other topics; hence, proposals ultimately have to be seen in their systematic unity. I trust that this initial bibliography shows that analytic philosophers have a contribution to make right across the board in theology.

There is one important complicating factor, namely, the terrain covered by prolegomenon. It is clear that work in this section of systematic theology traditionally spills over very quickly into a wide body of epistemological reflection. Too much recent theology has been captive to underdeveloped work in epistemology. For this reason I have become a keen advocate of the creation of a new sub-discipline within and between philosophy and theology that is best identified as the epistemology of theology.[2] I am convinced that until we shoulder this responsibility, work in theology will remain naïve about the options in epistemology for theology. Equally work in systematic theology will suffer from serious underdevelopment in its own right. So the section of prolegomenon is problematic. The solution to this problem here has been to cut back drastically on epistemological issues related to theology and to restrict the selection to material dealing potentially with the nature of analytic theology.

The choice of topics makes it clear that this bibliography deals essentially with topics in Christian theology. To some this will be a serious disappointment; they rightly and accurately point out that the work of analytic philosophers is also a resource for Jewish and Islamic theology. The answer to this disappointment is obvious. On the one hand, it is surely one of the great merits of analytic philosophy that its skills and virtues can indeed be deployed by Jewish and Islamic scholars. On the other hand, it is surely the task of Jewish and Islamic scholars to indicate how they want to proceed in their own versions of analytic theology; it would be both premature and presumptive for the Christian theologian to take on such an ambitious project at this time.

One last point: I am sure that there is excellent material that I have missed or overlooked in the compilation of this bibliography. I would be delighted if readers or authors would send me information about such material so that it may be incorporated into future editions.

---

[2] See the forthcoming volume edited by William J. Abraham and Frederick D. Aquino, *The Oxford Handbook of the Epistemology of Theology* (Oxford: Oxford University Press).

Systematic Theology as Analytic Theology[1]

William J. Abraham

Over its history systematic theology has delivered its goods under many names and in many forms. Generally the discipline has sought to provide a carefully constructed, coherent, interrelated articulation of Christian teaching that is apt for its particular time and space. However, the term is also used rather loosely. So systematic theology has been identified as dogmatic theology, constructive theology, and the interpretation of the Christian message. It has branded itself in terms of biblical theology, philosophical theology, existential theology, process theology, and the like. It has been linked to the achievement of great figures, as in Thomist theology, Calvinistic theology, and Wesleyan theology. Over the last two centuries it has been tied to various movements in Christianity such as liberal theology, evangelical theology, feminist theology, and liberation theology; or to various places as represented by Princeton theology, Third World theology, and the New Yale theology. Systematic theology has been a malleable and moveable feast that develops a great variety of modes of thought and sensibility. The emergence of systematic

[1] This essay is republished here by kind permission of Oxford University Press. Originally it was published in Oliver D. Crisp and Michael C. Rea (eds.), *Analytic Theology: New Essays in the Philosophy of Theology* (Oxford: Oxford University Press, 2009), 54-69.

theology as analytic theology was then an accident waiting to happen. Christian theologians have deployed the resources of many modes of philosophical thinking from the beginning; the turn to analytic philosophy as a source for systematic theology should neither surprise us nor initially trouble us.

In this paper I shall explore a vision of systematic theology as analytic theology, describe in general terms what that might involve, deal with some objections, and illustrate how it might proceed by taking up two loci of systematic theology and showing what analytic theology might look like in practice. I shall end with some suggestions on the division of labor between analytic theology and the epistemology of theology.

Analytic theology can usefully be defined as follows: it is systematic theology attuned to the deployment of the skills, resources, and virtues of analytical philosophy. It is the articulation of the central themes of Christian teaching illuminated by the best insights of analytic philosophy. One reason for proceeding with cautious cheerfulness in the development of analytic theology is that analytical philosophy, while it often deploys highly technical tools and skills, has from the beginning sought to illuminate our everyday concepts and modes of thought. To use the felicitous comment of Harry G. Frankfurt, "Surely one need not have been trained in any very distinctive philosophical tradition and skill in order to be able to think clearly, or reason carefully, and to keep one's eye on the ball."[2] This good sense can apply immediately to the prospects of analytical theology. To be sure, as analytic philosophy migrated and began exploring more specialized fields of discourse, say, in science, education, and history, philosophers of necessity

---

[2] Harry G. Frankfurt, *Necessity, Volition, and Love* (Cambridge: Cambridge University Press, 1999), p. xi.

had to be acquainted with what was going on in these domains. Yet the commitment to clarity and persuasive argument never wavered in this migration, and the fruits across the last century as seen in a host of disciplines have been intellectually invaluable.

The drive into theology is a natural one, even though some theologians are wont to complain that analytical philosophers are likely to oversimplify, to be historically insensitive, and to foster theological naiveté. The scattered work on Christian doctrine to date by philosophers gives cause for quiet optimism, for analytic philosophers of religion have been probing the contours and central themes of Christian theology for at least two generations. It would inflated to say that students in systematic theology would be delivered from many intellectual vices were they to be initiated into the rigors and clarity of analytic philosophy; analytical philosophy is not a holy laborsaving device, and analytic theology will no doubt have its own liabilities and vices. Yet the confusion that abounds in contemporary systematic theology is likely to diminish if theologians and their students come to terms with the virtues of the analytic tradition.[3]

As a discipline systematic theology has a set of topics or loci that are constitutive of its nature. While there are variations here and there, the set network of topics is

---

[3] The conceptual problems and intellectual sloppiness that bedevil contemporary systematic theology are highly visible in William C. Placher, ed., *Essentials of Christian Theology* (Louisville: Westminster/John Knox Press, 2003). This is one of the best readers currently available, yet one has only to compare it with standard readings in philosophy texts for undergraduate students to become aware of the difference in intellectual standards. It is pleasing to record an exception that proves the rule in John Webster, Kathryn Tanner, and Iain Torrance, eds., *The Oxford Handbook of Systematic Theology* (Oxford: Oxford University Press, 2007).

something like this: prolegomenon, the existence of God (attributes, Trinity), Christology, pneumatology, creation, providence, the human condition, ecclesiology, soteriology, and eschatology. The evidence for the claim that these topics and their internal themes represent the hard-drive of systematic theology is both empirical and normative. On the one hand, these are the topics that standard textbooks invariably take up and the conventional topics generally pursued by theologians. On the other hand, omission of any of these topics is a cause for substantial failure.[4]

These topics were clearly originally drawn from the great creeds or proto-creeds of the Church. They were not invented by theologians seeking tenure in the modern university. The first great systematic theologians, like Origen, the Cappadocians, and Augustine, were not starting from scratch in their work as theologians. They had already been baptized into the faith of the Church and found themselves driven by the inner logic of that faith to explore, expand, and enrich its central doctrines. They were engaged in a massive exercise of faith seeking understanding.

On the surface, dependence on the creeds as indispensable background music appears initially to be intellectually disastrous for analytic theology. It looks as if the early theologians were cooking the books in advance; and so the same criticism applies *mutatis mutandis* to the analytic theologian in relying on their

---

[4] *Essentials of Christian Theology*, for example, omits the whole topic of the Holy Spirit. Things fare even worse with Serene Jones and Paul Lakeland (eds.), *Constructive Theology* (Minneapolis: Fortress Press, 2005), which omits the sacraments, providence, the Trinity, and eschatology. As we shall see, great theologians like Jürgen Moltmann can get away with ignoring prolegomenon; this is a very illuminating omission of keen relevance to the work of analytic theology.

labors. Have we not already decided in favor of the truth of the faith? Is not theology a massive exercise in question-begging crucial truth claims that simply cannot be take for granted? Of course, if we define systematic theology in merely descriptive terms, this objection will not bother us. However, theologians have rightly been concerned with the truth of their claims rather than simply their authenticity or Christian identity. They have operated at the level of the normative and the prescriptive, seeking to articulate what we ought to believe rather than simply what has been believed. In other words, the task of apologetics and proof, while they have been conceived in radically different ways, has always been in the neighborhood. So the objection raised here has to be taken seriously; and I will return to this sort of query later.

Suffice it here to say that the worry initially is mere appearance. Conversion and baptism, where one encounters and receives the creed, were themselves a quest for truth. To be sure, it was a truth hidden from the world that had crucified in its earthy wisdom the Lord of Glory, but it was truth they had encountered, and it was truth that motivated their manifold labors.[5] Indeed the problem faced by the systematic theologian was how to come to terms with the truth of God revealed in Christ and brought home by the Holy Spirit. Systematic theology arose precisely because one had crossed over into the strange new world of the Church and the Bible and was compelled to think through systematically what one had gotten oneself into in one's Christian initiation. Within that initiation confession of the substance of the

---

[5] The truth of faith was not, of course, detached from participation in the life of God or from growth in sanctity, for it was truth that set the sinner free to discover their true destiny in creation and live a life of love to God and neighbor.

creeds as later canonically adopted at Nicea-Constantinople was not an optional issue; it was constitutive of baptism and conversion.

Donald Mackinnon captures both the challenge and commitment that stems from this feature of Christian existence.

> One who, like the present writer, is a professional philosopher is hardly likely to be tempted to underestimate the importance of the task of the Christian scholar. But it is, and must remain, a subordinate task, that is, to the proclamation of the everlasting Gospel of the mercy of God. It is always the temptation of the intellectual to resent the restriction laid upon him by the fact of the Gospel. To him the fact is scandalous, that is, a stumbling block, in a quite peculiar sense. Its 'fleshiness' oppresses him with an intensity that is manifested in the ingenuity wherewith he seeks to escape its burden. It is he who is aware of dogma (in the strict theological sense) as a restriction. Its presence inhibits him from erecting into an absolute a prevailing mood of thought. It is not those, who in the eyes of the world, are accounted poor and simple, that crave release from the cramping frame of Christian institutions. To them the giant affirmations of the Nicene Creed are not tiresome restraints imposed by an arbitrary authority. They are the lasting signpost to the fact that they were so loved by God that he gave them his only-begotten Son.[6]

Commitment to this kind of robust version of Christianity broke down in the modern period. In fact, the material content of systematic theology virtually disappeared in some quarters due to a Third Schism in the Church in which the canonical faith was deconstructed

---

[6] D. M. MacKinnon, *The Church* (London: Dacre Press, 1940), 50.

from within in the name of credibility and relevance.[7] The motives were good; theologians wanted to speak in a fitting manner to the intellectual and political challenges of the day. The problem was that so little doctrinal content was left by the time the theologians were finished speaking. This development in part explains the disarray within much contemporary systematic theology. If the deep truths of the Gospel and the central elements of the Nicene Creed are constitutive of the Christian faith, then much modern and contemporary theology is really the invention of various forms of post-Christian religion. Some theologians have, of course, been tempted to blame the breakdown within systematic theology on this or that philosopher or this or that philosophical mistake; but the role of philosophy in any proposed narrative of fall from grace is itself informed by philosophical judgment, so we should take the theological blame-game with a pinch of salt. The truth of the matter is complex, but there is no denying that the multiple attempts to revise the constitutive doctrines of Christianity have resulted in confusion and disarray within theology as an academic discipline. It is no surprise that theology has become thoroughly marginalized if not outright dismissed as a serious intellectual enterprise within the contemporary university.[8]

The issues at stake here are straightforwardly conceptual and spiritual. The Christian faith really does have a content that cannot be set aside without losing the faith itself. Given the concern about conceptual clarity within analytic theology, it is not at all surprising that

---

[7] I provide one narrative of this transition in *Canon and Criterion in Christian Theology* (Oxford: Clarendon, 1998).

[8] The issue is taken up with characteristic depth and originality by John Webster in *Theological Theology* (Oxford: Clarendon Press, 1998).

many talented analytical philosophers have gravitated towards robust forms of Christian theism. They do not want to be accused of not dealing with real Christianity; they have a sharp eye for equivocation and conceptual sleight of hand. Nor is it surprising that they have turned to doing theology themselves. They are intellectually and spiritually tired of been offered stones when they asked for bread.[9] It is true that, because of the theologically conservative cast of much analytical philosophy of religion, there has been a tension between theologians and philosophers that is not likely to dissolve in the near future. Theologians think that the philosophers are theologically naive;[10] philosophers think that theologians have given away the store for no good reason.[11] No doubt there is need for greater understanding on both sides of this divide. Analytical philosophers have had very good reasons for digging in on their side of the ditch; we can expect that much analytical theology will generally share this disposition.

[9] I recall vividly when I was a graduate student at Oxford attending during the same term the lectures of John Macquarrie and of A. J. Ayer. After complaining about the lack of substance and rigor in Macquarrie's lectures, I was chided by a friend from South Africa for my impatience and hasty judgments. So I repented and stayed the course. Three weeks later we left Macquarrie's lectures and, coming down the steps of Christ Church, I impishly said that if I had a choice between going to heaven with Macquarrie or to hell with A. J. Ayer, I was headed for hell. My friend immediately responded that he would be happy to come to hell with me.

[10] See, for example, Sarah Coakley, ' "Persons" in the "Social" Doctrine of the Trinity: A Critique of Current Analytic Discussion', in Stephen Davis, Daniel Kendall, and Gerald O'Collins, (eds.), *The Trinity* (Oxford: Oxford University Press, 1999), 123-44.

[11] See, for example, Alvin Plantinga, 'Sheehan's Shenanigans: How Theology Becomes Tomfoolery', in James F. Sennett, (ed.), *The Analytic Theis: An Alvin Plantinga Reader* (Grand Rapids: Eerdmans, 1998), 296-315.

However, this is not the whole story, for one can also read the development of analytic philosophy of religion and of analytic theology as a natural development from within philosophy itself. After the collapse of logical positivism with its strident polemic against the cognitive content of religious claims, a network of exceptionally able philosophers in Britain and North America took up philosophy of religion in the 1950s and 1960s in a way that forced others to take notice.[12] As philosophy of religion revived, more believers entered the profession; others came out of hiding; other philosophers bored by work in other fields and impressed by the freshness and boldness of the new work joined the fray as astute critics.[13] The result was an extraordinary renaissance of philosophy of religion that readily spilt over into work in philosophical theology and from thence over into theology proper.

I have already proposed an initial definition of analytic theology. It is systematic theology attuned to the deployment of the skills, resources, and virtues of analytical philosophy. This, of course, is just a beginning. How might we fruitfully proceed from here? One obvious way forward is to make some general comments on the nature of systematic theology developed with an analytic perspective. Beyond that we can look at some preliminary work on specific doctrines.

---

[12] Two collections of essays and two books became landmark texts: Antony Flew and Alasdair MacIntyre (eds.), *New Essays In Philosophical Theology* (London: SCM, 1995); Basil Mitchell (ed.), *Faith and Logic* (London: George Allen & Unwin, 1957); Alvin Plantinga, *God and Other Minds* (Ithica, NY: Cornell University Press, 1967); Basil Mitchell, *The Justification of Religious Belief* (London: Macmillan, 1973).

[13] See, for example, Richard M. Gale, *On the Existence and Nature of God* (Cambridge: Cambridge University Press, 1991).

First, analytical theology will put a high premium on conceptual clarity in exploring the doctrines take up within the various loci. Very generally this will mean coming clean on the concept of God at play throughout the loci. My own preference at this point is to conceive of God in terms of personal agency, rather than, say, Process, Being, the Absolute, and Spirit. In doing so I am not conceiving of God as simply a bigger and better version of human agents. At its core the idea of agency as applied to God signifies an agent who possesses all the standard attributes, who transcends space and time, and who exists in an utterly mysterious reality as three Persons in One Substance. The critical feature of agency in play here is that of acting on various intentions and purposes. We might say that God is that agent than which nothing greater can be thought, who has created and redeemed the world through His Son Jesus Christ in the activity of the Holy Spirit, and who will bring the redeemed creation to final glory in the future.

Second, analytical theology will naturally deploy the notion of narrative in spelling out the activity of God in creation and redemption. Beyond the ambivalent impact of Alasdair Macintyre this has not happened to date,[14] but it is easy to see why narrative is a crucial concept. The heart of Christian theology is a drama of creation, freedom, fall, and comprehensive renewal. Narrative matters at this point because it is through narrative, that

---

[14] Alasdair MacIntyre's stress on narrative in *After Virtue* (Notre Dame, Ind.: University of Notre Dame, 1981) and beyond has had a profound impact on contemporary theology through the work of Stanley Hauerwas and his students. However, MacIntyre, while his work clearly bears the hallmarks of analytic philosophy, has been scathing in his criticisms of analytic theology because of its lack of historical depth and sociological sensitivity; and Hauerwas, in part because of his strong Barthian sensibilities, has been reluctant to deploy the resources of analytical philosophy.

is, through the careful delineation of action, intention, and purpose, that the works of God are articulated and rendered intelligible.[15] Theological explanations are not scientific; they are inescapably personalistic and teleological; they involve personal causation rather than event causation. Narrative, to be sure, is a slippery notion so it can be deployed in a way that seeks to evade issues of truth and falsity. There is no equivocation at this point here; fictional and mythological narratives that carry deep theological truth are commonplace in the scriptures and the tradition of the Church; so there is no need to be squeamish or defensive about the complexity of narrative in the Christian tradition. However, the metanarrative of systematic theology is clearly intended to be read as true rather than as expressions of emotion, or as avowals to lead, say, an agapeistic way of life. It is the grand, reality-depicting narrative of creation, freedom, fall, and redemption that I have mind in when I suggest that analytic theology will take narrative with radical seriousness.

Third, analytical theology will bring to bear all the resources of conceptual clarification where appropriate to each of the doctrines articulated in the classical loci. It is hard to think of any doctrine from creation to eschatology where conceptual issues are not extremely important. It will be sufficient in a programmatic essay to draw attention to the kind of work that has already been done and further work that waits to be done in the future. For

---

[15] Contrary to what is widely held at the moment, this means that attempts to develop general theories of divine action yield only limited dividends in theology. A general theory of divine action does little to throw light on the meaning of specific action predicates as applied to God. What we need at this level is the creative deployment of analogical modes of thought that aptly explore how action predicates as applied to God do and do not match action predicates as applied to human agents.

the moment I shall eschew comments on issues in prolegomenon for reasons that will become clear later. But if we do not begin with prolegomenon, where can we begin?

Analytic theology can begin by standing inside the circle of Christian faith and seeking to articulate the deep contours of the vision of God that is to be found in the Church. We speak here unapologetically of the Christian God, the God of creation and redemption, whose saving acts are laid out in the Nicene Creed and in the manifold practices of the Church.[16] Within this horizon let me visit two distinct loci of systematic theology and see what emerges. I shall look at the doctrine of God and at the doctrine of grace and freedom. The aim overall is to indicate the kind of work that will come naturally to the analytic theologian.

Consider how analytic theology might proceed in articulating a robust doctrine of God. At present there is stout resistance in some theological circles to deploying philosophical skill in articulating a Christian vision of God that has multiple sources. There is, at the outset, the longstanding contrast that pits the god of the philosophers over against the God of Abraham, Isaac, and Jacob. From as far back as Tertullian and at least from Pascal onwards in the modern period we have been told that there is the dead, abstract god of the philosophers and the living God of scripture and faith.[17] Karl Barth's arguments against natural theology have aided and abetted this contrast sharply and made it the stable diet of three generations of theologians. To reach for the god of the philosophers is to

[16] For a delineation of what this means see William J. Abraham, Jason E. Vickers, and Natalie B. Van Kirk (eds.), *Canonical Theism* (Grand Rapids, Mich.: Eerdmans, 2008).
[17] For a recent expression of this tradition see Justo L. Gonzalez, *Mañana, Christian Theology from a Hispanic Perspective* (Nashville, Tenn.: Abingdon, 1990), ch. 6.

seek to justify ourselves by our works; it is to invent an idol rather than turn to the one true God of divine revelation; and it is to make revelation subordinate to human reason.[18] In addition it has been suggested from the side of recent liberation theology that the omnipotent, omniscient, omnipresent god of the philosophers is the top-down god of the masters, the god of empire.[19] An omnipotent god will end up, like it or not, being brought in to support the unilateral omnipotence of empire. Thus the god of the philosophers is, if only by default, in synch with the new North American, neo-colonial empire. From another angle the god of the philosophers is a god one comes to know through cold, clinical logic divorced from genuine spirituality and from the special revelation through whom God is supremely known and loved. So the god of the philosophers is really the god of pagan thinking rather than the God known and worshipped in the faith of the saints and martyrs.

These are certainly extremely interesting moves, but taken either singly or together they are not at all persuasive. On the contrary, we need the help of analytic theology to do justice to the God we meet in the worship of the Church. We can cut to the chase by noting that the God we have identified in our initial orientation is not some idol cooked up by philosophers, but precisely the God and Father of our Lord Jesus Christ, the Triune God of the Christian Creed and worship. The warrant for this move is simple: this is the way God is named and identified in the Church. To be sure this God can also be identified as the one and only Creator of the universe; and

---

[18] I have discussed this at greater length in *An Introduction to the Philosophy of Religion* (Englewood Cliffs, NJ: Prentice Hall, 1985), ch. 7.

[19] This is an important theme in Joerg Rieger, *Christ and Empire* (Minneapolis: Fortress, 2007), 240, 249, 254.

this God is also the God of Abraham, Isaac, and Jacob. However, our quarry is not the God of mere theism, but the God of the Gospel as identified and named over time in the Church canonically; it is the God of revelation, faith, and worship that matters in our doctrine of God. Thus the first task of a doctrine of God in analytic theology is to unpack as fully as possible what is involved in confessing that we believe in the Triune God of the Church. In doing so we can draw extensively on recent work on the nature of identity and we can explore metaphysical possibilities that would otherwise be overlooked or not taken seriously.[20]

What then about the classical attributes of God? Should these be included our doctrine of God? Are we not including alien material if we look at omnipotence, omniscience, omnipresence, and the like? If we deal with them at all, should we not confine ourselves to the sparse and meager references to them that show up in scripture? The response to this worry has long been available to us in the work of Anselm. Clearly Anselm began his thinking about God inside the faith. He was not in search of God or in search of a proof of God; he already had come to know God for himself in the life of the Church. What his stunning discovery in the *Proslogion* makes clear, however, is that the One he has encountered in the faith of the Church can also aptly be identified as nothing less than that than which nothing greater can be conceived. Hence in order to do justice to the God he knows and loves Anselm has judiciously hit upon a

[20] See, for example, Bruce M. Marshall, *Trinity and Truth* (Cambridge: Cambridge University Press, 2000), and Richard Swinburne, *The Christian God* (Oxford: Clarendon Press, 1994). For a penetrating discussion by a leading analytic philosopher on the doctrine of the Trinity see William P. Alston, 'Substance and the Trinity', in Stephen Davis, Daniel Kendall, and Gerald O'Collins (eds.), *The Trinity* (Oxford: Oxford University Press, 1999), 179-201.

conceptual means for expanding his vision of God. He is not just at liberty to explore the classical attributes of God as an exercise in abstract or mere semantics; he is required to stretch his mind to the limits in order to work out how he may now speak appropriately of God as omniscient, omnipotent, omnipresent, all-good, totally worthy of worship, and so on. In turn, this will require the analytic theologian to investigate how these attributes of God relate to God's work in creation, providence, and miracle, and to other relevant topics like natural and moral evil, human freedom, and God's sovereign control over all things.[21] At its limit Anselm eventually comes to the conclusion that the very idea of God requires his existence. This God is such that his non-existence is inconceivable; he differs so radically from all else in creation that he must exist.[22]

In my teaching of systematic theology to totally new believers in Kazakhastan I initially hesitated to introduce them to Anselm's vision of God. When I first did it, I noticed the lights go on in the mind of one of the brightest students present and asked afterwards why he was so excited about what had been said. He immediately replied that in thinking of God as that than which nothing greater can be conceived he had at long last found an apt way of describing that God of the Gospel who had saved his life and whom he gladly worshipped in the services of his local church. In this instance spirituality and theology were brought together in a pleasing harmony. I have seen this repeated again and again in my teaching of new converts in the Third World.

[21] For a fine exploration of these matters see Thomas V. Morris, *Our Idea of God* (Notre Dame, Ind.: University of Notre Dame, 1991).
[22] For a very important examination of this issue see Robert Prevost, *Probability and Theistic Explanation* (Oxford: Clarendon Press, 1990).

Moreover, we can add that to seek to prove the existence of this God in no way reduces God to an idol. The property of being proved is a Cambridge property; it takes nothing away from the subject in question. One can see this immediately by noting that proving that my daughter exists in no way turns her into an idol or diminishes my love and devotion towards her. Equally, it is inappropriate to confuse commitment to the God described in this robust Anselmic fashion with commitment to any political philosophy, whether to that of some empire or some other favored constituency. On the contrary, one can see how those committed to this vision of God are given resources to stand up to tyranny wherever it occurs. Commitment to a God who has entered into the brutality of human evil in the Cross and who is also omnipotent should be more than enough to provide lavish moral and spiritual resources in standing up to political and social evil.[23] So we can set aside the widespread aversion to putting rigorous philosophical analysis to work in exploring the rich contours of the Christian doctrine of God.

We can also begin to see how such analysis might help us both clarify and resolve a long-standing conundrum buried deep within the Christian doctrine of salvation. There are many elements at issue in the Christian doctrine of salvation. Initially they cluster in and around how to understand justification and sanctification. In turn these concepts open up the question of how we should think of the interrelation between divine and human action in salvation. One way to pose the issue is this: what is the relation between grace and freedom? On the one hand, we want to say that we are saved by grace; we

---

[23] For a stirring example of this see *Father Arseny, 1893-1973: Priest, Prisoner, Spiritual Father* (Crestwood, NY: St. Vladimir's Seminary Press, 2004).

depend on divine action to initiate, provide, and sustain the new life that Christ brings to us. There is no question of our being saved by our own works, by our own merit, or by our own worthiness. God alone saves us. On the other hand, we are not coerced into salvation; God does not save us against our wills; we are free to say no to God in salvation; and in the gospel we are called upon to repent, put our faith in Jesus Christ, to take up our crosses, to attend to the sacraments of the church, and the like. So how can we at one and the same time say that God alone saves us and that we have an indispensable role to play in the total process of salvation?

The Western tradition as a whole, following Augustine, has come heavily down on the side of grace. Grace operates from beginning to end; even the first move towards repentance is made possible by prevenient grace; and faith itself is a gift of God. This line has run so deep as to lead to the development of a vision of double, unconditional predestination in which God elects some to salvation and sees to it that they receive it and elects others to damnation and sees to it that they get what they deserve. This in turn has led either to a denial of freedom altogether or to compatibilist doctrines of freedom that do not baulk at insisting on divine determination of all that happens. While modern theologians are reluctant to go this far, the shadows of the logic of grace remain in the theological undergrowth and in much half-baked, popular piety. Any move to take seriously a more robust doctrine of freedom or to take seriously genuine human action in salvation will be greeted as a form of Pelagianism.

This is clearly one area where conceptual analysis is vital in unraveling the theological issues that need attention. To speak of grace is to enter the domain of causation. To say that we are saved by grace is to insist that we are saved by divine agency; we are explaining salvation in terms of the actions of God both in history and in the human soul. As J. R. Lucas has pointed out, however, it is easy at this point to be misled by the diverse way in which we use causal language.[24] Explanations are extraordinarily varied, but we can make progress by distinguishing two relevant types. There are those kinds of explanations where we supply full causal explanations of phenomena by means of natural laws and antecedent conditions. In this instance we are wedded to determinism; if we knew all the antecedent conditions and causal laws, then the outcome is determined. In these circumstances to explain the cause of what happened is to identify the complete cause. However, we also speak of causation in a quite different way, that is, we think of causation in terms of the most significant cause of the event in question. Here we select the cause of the event by picking out one factor as the critical factor, leaving aside for the moment all the other antecedent conditions that are pertinent. Thus we set aside standing conditions and negative conditions and focus in on this or that factor as the cause of what happened or what is going on. We do this most characteristically when we want to assign credit or responsibility to this or that causal agent.

With this distinction in hand we can begin to see what has gone astray in the debate about freedom and grace. What began as an effort to give credit to God in salvation has taken the language of most significant cause and stretched it to mean the complete cause. In the latter case there can be no room for human agency for the complete cause has been identified with God and the corollary of this is obvious: there can be no other causes, including human actions. Hence human agency must be eliminated completely or become so anemic as to be non-existent. Moreover, given the fat relentless human ego that is ever ready to take credit for anything we do, we are all too

---

[24] J. R. Lucas, *Freedom and Grace* (London: SPCK, 1976), 2.

ready to seize on any human action in salvation and construct grandiose schemes of credit and merit that quickly become schemes of salvation by works. In this instance the logic of our language and our sinful perversity feed off each other and the drift into Pelagianism becomes irresistible. However, once we trace the issue back to the complex causal and explanatory discourse that is operating as relevant background music, we can cut off such moves and begin to take seriously both genuine human freedom and agency in the total process of salvation. We are well on our way to solving the Augustinian-Pelagian controversy.

This conclusion will immediately seem far-fetched even to many analytic theologians; perhaps we have the glimmerings of a way forward rather than being well on our way to solving one of the deepest mysteries of the faith. Our optimism is a matter of degree at this point; for my part I am amazed at the progress that is already possible. However, I agree entirely that this optimism may be misplaced. Moreover, I also agree that there is much more to be done in the unraveling of this long-standing problem in Christian theology. We need a careful phenomenology of Christian conversion in all its teeming diversity. It is surely no accident that many are drawn to the Augustinian position because they are aware of how they were worn down by God in the journey home; without the relentless hound of heaven they would never have made it. However, we also need to look with care at other kinds of conversion narrative where the role of human action and the sense of human freedom are much more pronounced. In and around this we need a much more nuanced account of what is at stake in speaking of freedom or free will. It is clear that when Luther spoke of the bondage of the will he did not mean to treat human agents as mere mechanisms or automatons who acted out of total necessity. We can be in bondage to, say, bigotry or jealousy, and still be free to express our bigotry or jealousy in a host of ways. Likewise, there are a host of actions that we cannot will to do even though logically and humanly we are free to do them, as when we insist that we cannot do those things that run headlong into confrontation with those values and things we really care about.[25] So we need a much deeper account of the character of human agency and the dynamics of human action that crop up initially around disputes about free will. Finally, we need a more sensitive reading of the rhetoric involved in the call to human action and endeavor. When we tell our teenagers that they need to get their act together, that they can do much better than their current conduct suggests, we are not falling into a superficial vision of the human predicament. We are manifesting a complex interplay of human relations that have a genuine place for exhortation and inspiration. Likewise, when we are called upon to repent or to take up the cross, we are not falling into some kind of Pelagian doctrine of works righteousness. We are taking seriously the role of human response to the commands of God, even as, in those commands and exhortations, God is aiding us to do what we cannot do on our own.[26]

Thus far I have made some preliminary and descriptive comments about the nature of analytic theology and briefly explored what analytic theology might look like were it to take up the doctrine of God and the relation between grace and freedom. Yet plunging like this straight into the content of Christian theology may frustrate even the most sympathetic reader. What

---

[25] For an important treatment of this issue see Harry G. Frankfurt, *The Importance of What We Care About* (Cambridge: Cambridge University Press, 1988).
[26] I leave aside the need to develop an appropriate doctrine of sin, original and otherwise, at this point; but that issue too would benefit from careful philosophical analysis.

about the question of truth? What about the justification of these theological claims? What about the criteria of theological inquiry? Surely, it will be said, it is these questions that ought to be foremost in the work of analytic theology. In fact it seems perverse not to tackle these questions up front given that they are taken up within systematic theology itself in the opening section on prolegomenon. So why have I held back in raising them to this closing section?

It is certainly not because I think these questions unimportant. Nor am I belittling the wealth of recent work done on these issues by philosophers. My concerns are threefold. First, theologians become so consumed with epistemological issues that they never really get beyond the worries that arise once these issues are given a privileged position in the opening exercise in prolegomenon. Theologians never get over their initial doubts and skeptical impulses; and students become intellectually paralyzed and lose their confidence. Second, and alternatively, these questions are so difficult and complicated that it is very tempting for the theologian to reach for the nearest answer that lies to hand or to cut and paste this or that item in epistemology and hope that this will hit the target.[27] Either way, we are offered unsatisfactory solutions to a network of problems that deserve far more attention than can be given to them within the boundaries of a prolegomenon. Worse still, students offer up schoolboy solutions to problems in epistemology and develop a false sense of security in doing so. Third, as hinted earlier, the history of modern theology shows that a host of epistemologies deployed within prolegomenon have hindered rather than helped in

---

[27] Nowhere is this more visible than in the lazy and dogmatic use of the so-called Wesleyan quadrilateral of scripture, tradition, reason, and experience.

systematic theology. They have acted as a form of intellectual birth control in which the faith of the church has been prematurely aborted rather than allowed to come to full term. They operate as artificial and inappropriate forms of thought control within the borders of systematic theology.[28]

There is no easy solution to the problem I am identifying. Some theologians, like Jürgen Moltmann, have simply ignored it and left it to be taken up at the end of their careers. Others, like Barth, have realized the magnitude of the task and devoted hundreds of pages to tackling it, but then found themselves unable to finish their work. It is very tempting, of course, to hand the whole affair over to philosophy of religion and simply leave it at that. However, philosophers of religion all too often restrict themselves to the standard queries about the validity and soundness of natural theology and natural atheology and thus leave a host of important epistemological topics unattended.[29] Besides, they have

---

[28] It is clear, for example, that the restriction of warrant to religious experience has inhibited the development of robust doctrines of the Trinity, most famously in Fredrich Schleiermacher's great work in Christian theology, where the doctrine is relegated to an appendix. See *The Christian Faith* (Edinburgh: T. & T. Clark, 1928). The brilliant work of Schubert M. Ogden in the last generation also comes to mind, where similar effects can be seen in the field of Christology. See his *The Point of Christology* (Dallas, Tex.: Southern Methodist University Press, 1982). John Macquarrie's widely used *Principles of Christian Theology* (New York: Scribner, 1966, 1977) represents a similar trend where the constraints in this instance are derived from a heavy allegiance to a Heideggerian epistemology and ontology.

[29] It is rare nowadays to find the whole topic of revelation taken seriously; yet discussion of divine revelation is vital to the interests of systematic theology. For a fine exception see Sandra Lee Menssen and Thomas D. Sullivan, *The Agnostic Inquirer: Revelation from a Philosophical Standpoint* (Grand Rapids, Mich.: Eerdmans, 2007). It is clear that if it is the pure in heart who see God, then philosophers have

other issues to discuss. So this will only offer marginal assistance.

What we sorely need at this point is the creation of a new subdiscipline in the borderlands between philosophy and theology, namely, the epistemology of theology. What I envisage is a systematic, self-critical, historically informed inquiry into the epistemological issues that crop up in theology.[30] Such work will require the efforts of both philosophers and theologians; neither need confine themselves to the crumbs that fall from each other's tables; we need a new table where both can bring a full plate of food and their recipes to the feast. The theologians will be crucial because without them the subject matter of theology, namely, God, will never get the attention it deserves. The philosophers will be crucial because without them we will not have the full range of resources within epistemology at our disposal. Within this work we must let the subject matter of our inquiry in all its plenitude of being play a vital role in sorting out what counts as relevant evidence, justification, and warrant. Equally we must examine any and every proposal in this domain for its epistemological validity and fruitfulness. In doing so we are also under obligation to take up relevant matters about the nature of language and truth that naturally impinge on resolving epistemological questions that crop up within systematic theology. Nothing short of this, in my judgment, will

---

will need to pay attention to the place of the theological virtues of faith, hope, and love in discussions of the place of virtue epistemology in the epistemology of theology.

[30] Clearly this work will overlap with work that currently flies under the banner of "the epistemology of religious belief." The difference with this work will be two-fold: it will be confined to reflection of epistemological issues related to Christian theology (rather than to religion generally or to religions other than Christianity); and it will have space for the work of theologians as well as philosophers.

suffice to deal adequately with vital and inescapable questions on the nature of norm and truth that are currently sorted out in the prolegomena to systematic theology.[31]

Should we then reform systematic theology and eliminate the prolegomenon from systematic theology entirely? It is certainly tempting to take this step; there is a pleasing simplicity about this move. We could still, of course, retain an initial introductory section in which the analytic theologian provides relevant preliminary remarks to get the show up and running. "Prolegomenon" generally means quite simply the words that come at the beginning; so we can still use that term to cover an opening section that indicates the nature of the work to follow, the kind of questions that will be pursued, the assumptions that are already in play, and the like. We might even indicate in a cursory way the norms that will be deployed, noting that the full treatment of these matters must be taken up in their own right elsewhere. Such a move would dovetail nicely with the invention of a new section at the end, the postlegomenon, where we might take up again the bearing of our theological investigations on important questions in the epistemology of theology. This would be especially apt given that the analytic theologian will be deploying all sorts of arguments and reasons in working through those loci that rightly occupy the attention of the systematic theologian.

However we resolve the challenge of what we do in prolegomenon, we cannot cut and run when it comes to the central themes of systematic theology as these have been identified and explored across the centuries. The subject matter of systematic theology has its own

---

[31] I have pursued the epistemology of theology in *Crossing the Threshold of Divine Revelation* (Grand Rapids, Mich.: Eerdmans, 2006).

integrity. In the end the theologian must come to grips with the questions that arise in and around the activity of God in the great drama of creation, freedom, fall, and redemption. This is as true for analytic theology as it is for any other kind of theology. Within analytic theology the theologian will deploy the skills, resources, and virtues of analytic philosophy in clarifying and arguing for the truth of the Christian Gospel as taken up in the great themes of the creeds of the Church.[32] No doubt the analytic theologian can develop and display other interests and skills as garnered, say, from biblical studies, historical investigation, and cultural commentary. Moreover, there is no reason why the analytic theologian cannot keep an eye on the role of theology in the fostering of deep love for God; indeed that should be a concern of any theology whatever its virtues or vices.[33] There is ample evidence to hand to suggest that the time is ripe for the emergence of analytic theology; there is also sufficient evidence to suggest that this work will bear much fruit in the years ahead.

[32] For a fuller account of my own vision of the various tasks of systematic theology see my 'Canonical Theism and Systematic Theology', in *Canonical Theism*.
[33] For a point of entry into this arena see Robert C. Roberts, *Spiritual Emotions* (Grand Rapids, Mich.: Eerdmans, 2007).

1

Prolegomenon

Task, Method

Abraham, William J. "Philosophy of Religion." In *An Introduction to the Philosophy of Religion,* by William J. Abraham. Englewood Cliffs: Prentice-Hall, 1985, 1-11.

———. "Systematic Theology as Analytic Theology." In *Analytic Theology: New Essays in the Philosophy of Theology,* edited by Oliver D. Crisp and Michael C. Rea. Oxford: Oxford University Press, 2009, 54-69.

Beilby, James K. "Introduction: The Contribution of Philosophy to Theology." In *For Faith and Clarity: Philosophical Contributions to Christian Theology,* edited by James K. Beilby. Grand Rapids: Baker Academic, 2006, 13-24.

Clark, Kelly James. *Philosophers Who Believe: The Spiritual Journeys of 11 Leading Thinkers.* Downers Grove: InterVarsity Press, 1993.

Coakley, Sarah. "Feminism and Analytic Philosophy of Religion." In *The Oxford Handbook of Philosophy of Religion,* edited by William J. Wainwright. New York: Oxford University Press, 2005, 494-526.

―――. "Why Analytic Theology is Not a Club." *Journal of the American Academy of Religion*, forthcoming.

Crisp, Oliver D. "Analytic Philosophy." In *Theology and Philosophy, Faith and Reason*, edited by Oliver D. Crisp, Gavin D'Costa, Mervyn Davies, and Peter Hampson. New York: Continuum, 2012, 171-185.

―――. "On Analytic Theology." In *Analytic Theology: New Essays in the Philosophy of Theology*, edited by Oliver D. Crisp and Michael C. Rea. Oxford: Oxford University Press, 2009, 33-53.

Davis, Stephen T. "Revelation and Inspiration." In *The Oxford Handbook of Philosophical Theology*, edited by Thomas P. Flint and Michael C. Rea. Oxford: Oxford University Press, 2009, 30-53.

Donagan, Alan. "Can Anybody in a Post-Christian Culture Rationally Believe the Nicene Creed." In *Reflections on Philosophy and Religion*, by Alan Donagan, edited by Anthony N. Perovich. New York: Oxford University Press, 1999, 15-34.

―――. "Philosophy and the Possibility of Religious Orthodoxy." In *Reflections on Philosophy and Religion*, by Alan Donaga, edited by Anthony N. Perovich. New York: Oxford University Press, 1999, 3-14.

Engelhardt, H. Tristram, Jr. "Critical Reflections on Theology's Handmaid: Why the Role of Philosophy in Orthodox Christianity is so Different." *Philosophy and Theology* 18, no. 1 (2006): 53-75.

Evans, Stephen C. "Faith and Revelation." In *The Oxford Handbook of Philosophy of Religion*, edited by William J. Wainwright. Oxford: Oxford University Press, 2005, 323-343.

———. "On Taking God Seriously." In *God, Philosophy and Academic Culture*, edited by William J. Wainwright. Atlanta: Scholars Press, 1996, 59-70.

Farrer, Austin. "A Starting-point for the Philosophical Examination of Theological Belief." In *Faith and Logic: Oxford Essays in Philosophical Theology*, edited by Basil Mitchell. London: George Allen & Unwin, 1958, 9-30.

Griffiths, Paul J. "Culture's Catechumens and the Church's Task." In *Handing on the Faith: The Church's Mission and Challenge,* edited by Robert P. Imbelli. New York: Herder & Herder, 2006, 44-59.

———. "From Curiosity to Studiousness: Catechizing the Appetite for Knowledge."In *Faith, Learning, and Christian Practices,* edited by D. Smith and J. Smith. Grand Rapids, Michigan: Eerdmans, 2011, 102-122.

———. "Which Are the Words of Scripture?" *Theological* Studies 72 (2011), 703-722.

Hasker, William. "Analytic Philosophy of Religion." In *The Oxford Handbook of Philosophy of* Religion, edited by William J. Wainwright. New York: Oxford University Press, 2007, 421-446.

Jones, Joe R. *A Grammar of Christian Faith: Systematic Explorations in Christian Life and Doctrine* (2 Volume Set). Lanham, Md: Rowman & Littlefield, 2002.

Kaufman, Gordon D. *An Essay on Theological Method.* Atlanta: Scholars Press, 1995.

Louth, Andrew. *Theology and Spirituality.* Fairacres, Oxford: SLG Press, 1978. Note: This paper was first read to the Origen Society on 30 October 1974

Mackey, Louis. "Redemptive Subversions: the Christian Discourse of St. Bonaventure." In *The Autonomy of Religious Belief: A Critical Inquiry,* edited by Frederick James Crosson. Notre Dame: University of Notre Dame Press, 1981, 38-59.

Marshall, Bruce D. "Absorbing the World: Christianity and the Universe of Truths" as well as "Introduction." In *Theology and Dialogue: Essays in Conversation with George Lindbeck,* edited by Bruce D. Marshall. Notre Dame: University of Notre Dame Press, 1990), 69-102, 1-4.

———. "Analogie II: fundamentaltheologisch; III: religionsphilosophisch," *Die Religion in Geschichte und Gegenwart,* 4th edition, vol. 1 (Tübingen: Mohr Siebeck, 1998), 448-51.

———. "Christ the End of Analogy" In *The Analogy of Being: Invention of the Antichrist or the Wisdom of God?,* edited by Thomas Joseph White. Grand Rapids: Eerdmans, 2011, 280-313.

———. "Meaning and Truth in Narrative Interpretation: A Reply to George Schner." *Modern Theology* 8, no. 2 (1992), 173-9.

———. "Philosophy and Theology." In *The Encyclopedia of Christianity Vol. 4, P-Sh,* edited by

Erwin Fahlbusch and G. W. Bromiley. Grand Rapids [etc.]: Eerdmans, 2005, 195-200.

————. "*Quod Scit Una Uetula*: Aquinas on the Nature of Theology," In *The Theology of Thomas Aquinas*, edited by Rik Van Nieuwenhove and Joseph Wawrykow. Notre Dame: University of Notre Dame Press, 2005, 1-35.

————. "Scholasticism." In *The Encyclopedia of Christianity Vol. 4, P-Sh,* edited by Erwin Fahlbusch and G. W. Bromiley. Grand Rapids [etc.]: Eerdmans, 2005, 863-70.

————. "'We Shall Bear the Image of the Man of Heaven': Theology and the Concept of Truth." *Modern Theology* 11, no. 1 (1995), 93-117; also in *Rethinking Metaphysics,* edited by L. Gregory Jones and Stephen E. Fowl. Oxford: Blackwell, 1995. 93-117.

Mitchell, Basil. "Introduction." In *Faith and Logic: Oxford Essays in Philosophical Theology,* edited by Basil Mitchell. London: Allen & Unwin, 1958, 1-8.

Moreland, J. P. "General Ontology and Theology: A Primer." In *For Faith and Clarity: Philosophical Contributions to Christian Theology,* edited by James K. Beilby. Grand Rapids: Baker Academic, 2006, 45-64.

Morris, Thomas V. *God and the Philosophers: The Reconciliation of Faith and Reason.* New York: Oxford University Press, 1994.

Moser, Paul K. "Jesus on Knowledge of God." *Christian Scholars Review*, Vol. 28, no. 4 (1999), 586-604.

Padgett, Alan. "The Relationship between Theology and Philosophy: Constructing a Christian Worldview." In *For Faith and Clarity: Philosophical Contributions to Christian Theology*, edited by James K. Beilby. Grand Rapids: Baker Academic, 2006, 25-45.

Plantinga, Alvin. "Prologue: Advice to Christian Philosophers." In *Christian Theism and the Problems of Philosophy*, edited by Michael D. Beaty. Notre Dame: University of Notre Dame Press, 1990.

Rauser, Randal. "Theology as a Bull Session." In *Analytic Theology: New Essays in the Philosophy of Theology*, edited by Oliver D. Crisp and Michael C. Rea. Oxford: Oxford University Press, 2009, 70-86.

Reno. R. R. "Theology's Continental Captivity." *First Things* 162 (April 2006), 26-33.

Stroll, Avrum. *Twentieth Century Analytic Philosophy*. New York: Columbia University Press, 2000.

Stump, Eleonore. "Revelation and Biblical Exegesis: Augustine, Aquinas, and Swinburne." In *Reason and the Christian Religion: Essays in Honour of Richard Swinburne*, edited by Alan G. Padgett. Oxford: Clarendon Press, 1994, 161-197.

Swinburne, Richard. "Authority of Scripture, Tradition, and the Church." In *The Oxford Handbook of Philosophical Theology*, edited by Thomas P. Flint and Michael C. Rea. Oxford: Oxford University Press, 2009, 11–29.

Taliaferro, Charles. "Religious Beliefs." Chap. 1 in *Contemporary Philosophy of Religion*, by Charles Taliaferro. Malden: Blackwell, 1998, 14-35.

Wainwright, William J. "Theology and Mystery." In *The Oxford Handbook of Philosophical Theology*, edited by Thomas P. Flint and Michael C. Rea. Oxford: Oxford University Press, 2009, 78–102.

Wolterstorff, Nicholas. "How Philosophical Theology Became Possible within the Analytic Tradition of Philosophy." In *Analytic Theology: New Essays in the Philosophy of Theology*, edited by Oliver D. Crisp and Michael C. Rea. Oxford: Oxford University Press, 2009, 155-170.

2

God

Trinity, Attributes, Divine agency/action

Trinity

Alston, William P. "Substance and the Trinity." In *The Trinity: An Interdisciplinary Symposium on the Trinity,* edited by Stephen T. Davis, Daniel Kendall, and Gerald O'Collins. Oxford: Oxford University Press, 1999, 179-201.

Barnes, Michel René. "Rereading Augustine's Theology of the Trinity." In *The Trinity: An Interdisciplinary Symposium on the Trinity,* edited by Stephen T. Davis, Daniel Kendall, and Gerald O'Collins. Oxford: Oxford University Press, 1999, 145-176.

Brower, Jeffrey E. and Michael C. Rea. "Material Constitution and the Trinity." In *Oxford Readings in Philosophical Theology: Vol. 1: Trinity, Incarnation, and Atonement,* edited by Michael C. Rea. Oxford: Oxford University Press, 2009, 127-150.

Brown, David. "Trinitarian Personhood and Individuality." In *Trinity, Incarnation, and Atonement: Philosophical and Theological Essays,* edited by Ronald Jay Feenstra and Cornelius Plantinga. Notre Dame: University of Notre Dame Press, 1989, 48-78.

———. "Trinity." In *A Companion to Philosophy of Religion*, edited by Philip L. Quinn and Charles Taliaferro. Cambridge, Mass: Blackwell Publishers, 1999, 525-531.

Coakley, Sarah. "God as Trinity: An Approach through Prayer." In *We Believe in God,* Doctrine Commission of the Church of England. London: Church House Publishing, 1987, 104–121.

———. "Introduction: Disputed Questions in Patristic Trinitarianism." In *The God of Nicaea: Disputed Questions in Patristic Trinitarianism*, edited by Sarah Coakley, special guest-edited issue of *Harvard Theological Review* 100 (2007), 125–138.

———. "Living into the Mystery of the Holy Trinity: Trinity, Prayer, and Sexuality." *The Anglican Theological Review* 80 (1998), 223–32, also in slightly revised form as "The Trinity, Prayer and Sexuality: A Neglected Nexus in the Fathers and Beyond." *Centro Pro Unione* 58 (2000), 13–17; and anthologized in shortened form in *Feminism and Theology,* edited by Janet Martin Soskice and Diana Lipton. Oxford: Oxford University Press, 2003, 258–267.

——— "'Persons' in the 'Social' Doctrine of the Trinity: A Critique of Current Analytic Discussion." In *The Trinity: An Interdisciplinary Symposium on the Trinity,* edited by Stephen T. Davis, Daniel Kendall, and Gerald O'Collins. Oxford: Oxford University Press, 1999, 123-144.

———. "'Persons.' in the 'Social' Doctrine of the Trinity: Current Analytic Discussion and 'Cappadocian' Theology." In *Powers and Submissions: Spirituality, Philosophy, and Gender*. Oxford: Blackwell Publishers, 2002, 109-129.

———. "The Trinity and Gender Reconsidered." In *God's Life in Trinity (a Festschrift for Jürgen Moltmann)*, edited by Miroslav Volf and Michael Welker. Minneapolis: Fortress, 2006, 133-142.

———. "What Does Chalcedon Solve and What Does it Not? Some Reflections on the Status and Meaning of the Chalcedonian 'Definition.'" In *The Incarnation: An Interdisciplinary Symposium on the Incarnation of the Son of God*, edited by Stephen T. Davis, Daniel Kendall and Gerald O'Collins. Oxford: Oxford University Press, 2002, 143-163.

———. "Why Three? Some Further Reflections on the Doctrine of the Trinity." In *The Making and Remaking of Christian Doctrine: Essays in Honour of Maurice Wiles*, edited by Sarah Coakley and Daviv A. Pailin. Oxford: Oxford University Press, 1993, 29-56.

Cross, Richard. "Two Models of the Trinity?" In *Oxford Readings in Philosophical Theology, Vol. 1, Trinity, Incarnation, and Atonement*, edited by Michael C. Rea. Oxford: Oxford University Press, 2009, 107-126.

Del Colle, Ralph. "The Triune God." In *The Cambridge*

Companion to Christian Doctrine, edited by Colin E. Gunton. Cambridge: Cambridge University Press, 1997, 121-140.

Durand, Emmanual. "A Theology of God the Father." In *The Oxford Handbook of the Trinity,* edited by Gilles Emery and Matthew Levering. Oxford: Oxford University Press, 2011, 371-386.

Forrest, Peter. "Divine Fission: A New Way of Moderating Social Trinitarianism." In *Oxford Readings in Philosophical Theology: Vol. 1: Trinity, Incarnation, and Atonement,* edited by Michael C. Rea. Oxford: Oxford University Press, 2009, 44-60.

Holzer, Vincent. "Karl Rahner, Hans Urs von Balthasar, and Twentieth-Century Catholic Currents on the Trinity." In *The Oxford Handbook of the Trinity,* edited by Gilles Emery and Matthew Levering. Oxford: Oxford University Press, 2011, 314-327.

Hunsinger, George. "Karl Barth's Doctrine of the Trinity, and Some Protestant Doctrines after Barth." In *The Oxford Handbook of the Trinity,* edited by Gilles Emery and Matthew Levering. Oxford: Oxford University Press, 2011, 294-313.

Kerr, Fergus. "Trinitarian Theology in the Light of Analytic Philosophy." In *The Oxford Handbook of the Trinity,* edited by Gilles Emery and Matthew Levering. Oxford: Oxford University Press, 2011, 339-348.

Leftow, Brian. "Anti Social Trinitarianism." In *The Trinity: An Interdisciplinary Symposium on the Trinity,* edited by Stephen T. Davis, Daniel Kendall, and Gerald O'Collins. Oxford: Oxford University Press, 1999, 203-250.

———. "A Latin Trinity." In *Oxford Readings in Philosophical Theology: Vol. 1: Trinity, Incarnation, and Atonement*, edited by Michael C. Rea. Oxford: Oxford University Press, 2009, 76-106.

———. "Modes without Modalism." In *Persons: Human and Divine*, edited by Peter Van Inwagen and Dean W. Zimmerman. Oxford: Clarendon, 2007, 357-375.

Marshall, Bruce D. "Aquinas the Augustinian? On the Uses of Augustine in Aquinas's Trinitarian Theology." In *Aquinas the Augustinian*, edited by Michael Dauphinais, Barry David, and Matthew Levering. Washington, D.C.: Catholic University of America Press, 2007, 41-61.

———. "The Defense of the *Filioque* in Classical Lutheran Theology: An Ecumenical Appreciation." *Neue Zeitschrift für systematische Theologie und Religionsphilosophie* 44, no. 2 (2002), 154-73.

———. "The Filioque as Theology and Doctrine: In Reply to Bernd Oberdorfer." *Kerygma und Dogma* 50, no. 4 (2004), 271-88.

———. "In Search of an Analytic Aquinas: Grammar and the Trinity." In *Grammar and Grace: Reformulations of Aquinas and Wittgenstein*, edited by Jeffrey Stout and Robert MacSwain. London: SCM, 2004, 55-74.

——— "The Trinity." In *The Blackwell Companion to Modern Theology*, edited by Gareth Jones. Oxford: Blackwell, 2004, 183-203.

————."The Trinity" In *The Cambridge History of Later Medieval Theology*, edited by Joseph Wawrykow and Thomas Prügl. Cambridge: Cambridge University Press, forthcoming.

————. "Putting Shadows to Flight: The Trinity, Faith, and Reason." In *Reason and the Reasons of Faith*, edited by Paul J. Griffiths and Reinhard Hütter. New York: T. & T. Clark, 2005), 53-77.

————. "The Unity of the Triune God: Reviving an Ancient Question," *The Thomist* 74 (2010), 1-32.

————."*Utrum Essentia Generet*: Semantics and Metaphysics in Later Medieval Trinitarian Theology." In *Trinitarian Theology in the Medieval West*, edited by Pekka Kärkkäinen. Helsinki: Luther-Agricola-Soc., 2008, 88-123.

Martinich, A.P. "Identity and Trinity." *Journal of Religion* 58 (1978): 169-81.

Moreland, J. P. and William Lane Craig. "The Trinity." In *Oxford Readings in Philosophical Theology: Vol. 1: Trinity, Incarnation, and Atonement*, edited by Michael C. Rea. Oxford: Oxford University Press, 2009, 21-44.

Plantinga, Cornelius. "Social Trinity and Tritheism." In *Trinity, Incarnation, and Atonement: Philosophical and Theological Essays,* edited, Ronald Jay Feenstra and Cornelius Plantinga. Notre Dame: University of Notre Dame Press, 1989, 21-47.

Rahner, Karl. "Trinity, Divine." In *Encyclopedia of Theology: The Concise Sacramentum Mundi*, edited by Karl Rahner. London: Burns and Oates, 1975, 1755-1764.

Rauser, Randal. "Rahner's Rule: An Emperor Without Clothes." *International Journal of Systematic Theology* 7, no. 1 (January 2005), 81-94.

Rea, Michael C. "The Trinity." In *The Oxford Handbook of Philosophical Theology*, edited by Thomas P. Flint and Michael C. Rea. Oxford: Oxford University Press, 2009, 403-429.

Sanders, Fred. "The Trinity." In *The Oxford Handbook of Systematic Theology,* edited by J. B. Webster, Kathryn Tanner, and Iain R. Torrance. Oxford: Oxford University Press, 2007, 35-53.

Soskice, Janet Martin. "Trinity and the 'Feminine Other.'" In *The Kindness of God: Metaphor, Gender, and Religious Language* by Janet Martin Soskice. Oxford: Oxford University Press, 2007, 100-124.

———. "The Kindness of God: Trinity and the Image of God in Julian of Norwich and Augustine." In *The Kindness of God: Metaphor, Gender, and Religious Language* by Janet Martin Soskice. Oxford: Oxford University Press, 2007, 125-156.

Stump, Eleonore. "Francis and Dominic: Persons, Patterns, and Trinity." *American Catholic Philosophical Quarterly*, Proceedings of the American Catholic Philosophical Association issue, 74 (2000), 1-25.

Swinburne, Richard. *The Christian God*. Oxford: Clarendon Press, 1994.

Tanner, Kathryn E. "The Trinity as Christian Teaching." In *The Oxford Handbook of the Trinity*, edited by Gilles Emery and Matthew Levering. Oxford: Oxford University Press, 2011, 349-358.

————."Social Trinitarianism and its Critics." in *Rethinking Trinitarian Theology: Disputed Questions and Contemporary Issues in Trinitarian Theology*, edited by Giulio Maspero and Robert Józef Wozniak. London: T & T Clark, 2012, 368-386.

Te Velde, Rudi A. "The Divine Prson(s): Trinity, Person, and A nalogous Naming." In *The Oxford Handbook of the Trinity*, edited by Gilles Emery and Matthew Levering. Oxford: Oxford University Press, 2011, 359-370.

Tracy, David. "Trinitarian Speculation and the Forms of Divine Disclosure." In *The Trinity: An Interdisciplinary Symposium on the Trinity*, edited by Stephen T. Davis, Daniel Kendall, and Gerald O'Collins. Oxford: Oxford University Press, 1999, 273-294.

Van Inwagen, Peter. "Not by Confusion of Substance, but by Unity of Person." In *Reason and the Christian Religion: Essays in Honour of Richard Swinburne*, edited by Alan G. Padgett. Oxford: Clarendon Press, 1994, 201-226.

————. "Three Persons in One Being." In *Oxford Readings in Philosophical Theology, Vol. 1, Trinity, Incarnation, and Atonement*, edited by Michael C. Rea. Oxford: Oxford University Press, 2009, 61-75.

Volf, Miroslav and Michael Welker, editors. *God's Life in Trinity*. Minneapolis: Fortress Press, 2006.

Weinandy, Thomas G. "Trinitarian Christology: The Eternal Son." In *The Oxford Handbook of the Trinity*, edited by Gilles Emery and Matthew Levering. Oxford: Oxford University Press, 2011, 387-389.

Williams, C. J. F. "Neither Confounding the Persons nor Dividing the Substance." In *Reason and the Christian Religion: Essays in Honour of Richard Swinburne,* edited by Alan G. Padgett. Oxford: Clarendon Press, 1994, 227-243.

Wren-Lewis, John. "Modern Philosophy and the Doctrine of the Trinity." *The Philosophical Quarterly*, 5 (1955), 214-224.

Yandell, Keith. "Ontological Arguments, Metaphysical Identity, and the Trinity." In *Philosophia Christi*. Edited by Craig J. Hazen. Series 2, vol. 1, no. 1 (1999).

Attributes

Adams, Robert Merrihew. "Divine Necessity." In *The Virtue of Faith and Other Essays in Philosophical Theology,* by Robert Adams. New York: Oxford University Press, 1987, 209-220.

Alston, William P. "Divine Foreknowledge and Alternative Conceptions of Human Freedom. In *Divine Nature and Human Language: Essays in*

Philosophical Theology, by William P. Alston. Ithaca: Cornell University Press, 1989,162-177.

————. "Divine-human Dialogue and the Nature of God." In *Divine Nature and Human Language: Essays in Philosophical Theology,* by William P. Alston. Ithaca: Cornell University Press, 1989,144-161.

————. "Does God have Beliefs." In *Divine Nature and Human Language: Essays in Philosophical Theology,* by William P. Alston. Ithaca: Cornell University Press, 1989, 178-196.

Basinger, David. *Divine Power in Process Theism: A Philosophical Critique.* Albany: SUNY Press, 1988.

Beilby, James K. and Paul R. Eddy editors. *Divine Foreknowledge: Four Views.* Downers Grove: InterVarsity Press, 2001.

Brink, Gijsbert van den, and Marcel Sarot, editors. *Understanding the Attributes of God.* Frankfurt am Main: P. Lang, 1999.

Brower, Jeffrey E. "Simplicity and Aseity." In *The Oxford Handbook of Philosophical Theology*, edited by Thomas P. Flint and Michael C. Rea. Oxford: Oxford University Press, 2009, 105-128.

Craig, William Lane. "Divine Eternity." In *The Oxford Handbook of Philosophical Theology*, edited by Thomas P. Flint and Michael C. Rea. Oxford: Oxford University Press, 2009, 145-166.

————. "Pantheists in Spite of Themselves: God and Infinity in Contemporary Theology." In *For Faith and Clarity: Philosophical Contributions to*

Christian Theology, edited by James K. Beilby. Grand Rapids: Baker Academic, 2006, 135-156.

Creel, Richard E. *Divine Impassibility: An Essay in Philosophical Theology*. Cambridge: Cambridge University Press, 1986.

———. "Immutability and Impassibility." In *A Companion to Philosophy of Religion*, edited by Philip L. Quinn and Charles Taliaferro. Cambridge, Mass: Blackwell, 1999, 313-322.

Crombie, I. M. "Eternity and Omnitemporality." In *The Rationality of Religious Belief: Essays in Honour of Basil Mitchell*, edited by William J. Abraham and Steven W. Holtzer. Oxford: Oxford University Press, 1987, 169-188.

Davies, Brian. "Simplicity." In *The Cambridge Companion to Christian Philosophical Theology*, edited by Charles Taliaferro and Chad V. Meister. Cambridge: Cambridge University Press, 2010, 31-45.

Davis, Stephen T. *Logic and the Nature of God*. Grand Rapids, Mich: W.B. Eerdmans Pub. Co, 1983.

Fischer, John Martin. "Molinism." In *Oxford Studies in Philosophy of Religion, Vol. 1*, edited by Jonathan L. Kvanvig. Oxford: Oxford University Press 2008, 18-43.

Flint, Thomas P., and Alfred J. Freddoso. "Maximal Power." In *The Existence and Nature of God*, edited by Alfred J. Freddoso. Notre Dame: University of Notre Dame Press, 1983, 81-113.

Garcia, Laura. "Moral Perfection." In *The Oxford Handbook of Philosophical Theology*, edited by Thomas P. Flint and Michael C. Rea. Oxford: Oxford University Press, 2009, 217-240.

Gavriljuk, Pavel L. *The Suffering of the Impassible God: The Dialectics of Patristic Thought*. Oxford: Oxford Univ. Press, 2004.

Griffiths, Paul J. "Buddha and God: A Contrastive Study in Ideas About Maximal Greatness." *Journal of Religion* 69 (1989), 502-529. Reprinted in *Indian Philosophy: Philosophy of Religion,* edited by Roy W. Perrett. New York & London: Garland Publishing, 2001, 132-159.

Hare, John E. "Goodness." In *The Cambridge Companion to Christian Philosophical Theology,* edited by Charles Taliaferro and Chad V. Meister. Cambridge: Cambridge University Press, 2010, 66-80.

Hasker, William. "Eternity and Providence." In *The Cambridge Companion to Christian Philosophical Theology,* edited by Charles Taliaferro and Chad V. Meister. Cambridge: Cambridge University Press, 2010, 81-94.

———. *God, Time, and Knowledge*. Ithaca: Cornell University Press, 1989.

Helm, Paul. "Anselm's Proslogion." In *Faith and Understanding* by Paul Helm. Grand Rapids, Mich: Wm. B. Eerdmans Pub, 1997.

————. "Divine Foreknowledge and Fatalism." In *Eternal God: A Study of God Without Time* by Paul Helm. Oxford: Clarendon Press, 1988, 126-143.

————. "Goodness." In *A Companion to Philosophy of Religion,* edited by Philip L. Quinn and Charles Taliaferro. Cambridge, Mass: Blackwell, 1999, 243-249.

————. "Timelessness and Human Responsibility." In Paul Helm, *Eternal God: A Study of God Without Time.* Oxford: Clarendon Press, 1988, 144-170.

Hoffman, Joshua, and Gary Rosenkrantz. "Omnipotence." In *A Companion to Philosophy of Religion,* edited by Philip L. Quinn and Charles Taliaferro. Cambridge, Mass: Blackwell, 1999, 229-235.

Holmes, Stephen R. "The Attributes of God." In *The Oxford Handbook of Systematic Theology,* edited by J. B. Webster, Kathryn Tanner, and Iain R. Torrance. Oxford: Oxford University Press, 2007, 54-71.

Hudson, Hud. "Omnipresence." In *The Oxford Handbook of Philosophical Theology*, edited by Thomas P. Flint and Michael C. Rea. Oxford: Oxford University Press, 2009, 199-216.

Kenny, Anthony. *The God of the Philosophers*. Oxford: Clarendon Press, 1979.

Leftow, Brian. "Aquinas, Divine Simplicity and Divine Freedom." In *Metaphysics and God: Essays in Honor of Eleonore Stump*, edited by Kevin Timpe. New York: Routledge, 2009, 21-38.

————. "Eternity." In *A Companion to Philosophy of Religion,* edited by Philip L. Quinn and Charles Taliaferro. Cambridge, Mass: Blackwell, 1999, 257-264.

————. Necessity." In *The Cambridge Companion to Christian Philosophical Theology,* edited by Charles Taliaferro and Chad V. Meister. Cambridge: Cambridge University Press, 2010, 15-30.

————. "Omnipotence." In *The Oxford Handbook of Philosophical Theology*, edited by Thomas P. Flint and Michael C. Rea. Oxford: Oxford University Press, 2009, 167-198.

————. *Time and Eternity*. Ithaca: Cornell University Press, 1991.

Lewis, C. S. "Divine Goodness." In *The Problem of Pain* by C. S. Lewis. San Francisco: HarperSanFrancisco, 2001, 28-47.

Mann, William E. "The Metaphysics of Divine Love." In *Metaphysics and God: Essays in Honor of Eleonore Stump*, edited by Kevin Timpe. New York: Routledge, 2009, 60-75.

————. "Necessity." In *A Companion to the Philosophy of Religion,* edited by Philip L. Quinn and Charles Taliaferro. Cambridge, Mass: Blackwell, 1997, 264-270.

Marshall, Bruce D. "The Dereliction of Christ and the Impassibility of God," In *Divine Impassibility and the Mystery of Human Suffering*, edited by James Keating and Thomas Joseph White. Grand Rapids: Eerdmans, 2009, 246-298.

Mavrodes, George I. "How Does God Know the Things He Knows?" In *Divine and Human Action: Essays in the Metaphysics of Theism,* edited by Thomas V. Morris. Ithaca: Cornell University Press, 1988, 345-362.

————. "Omniscience." In *A Companion to Philosophy of Religion,* edited by Philip L. Quinn and Charles Taliaferro. Cambridge, Mass: Blackwell, 1999, 236-242.

————. "Proofs of God's Existence." In *Belief in God: A Study in the Epistemology of Religion* by George I. Mavrodes. Washington D.C.: University Press of America, 1970.

Morris, Thomas V. *Our Idea of God: An Introduction to Philosophical Theology.* Downers Grove, Ill: InterVarsity Press, 1991.

Nissing, Hanns-Gregor. *Sprache als Akt bei Thomas von Aquin.* Leiden: Brill, 2006.

Plantinga, Alvin. "Does God Have a Nature?" In *The Analytic Theist: An Alvin Plantinga Reader,* edited by James F. Sennett. Grand Rapids: Eerdmans, 1998, 225-257.

————. *Does God Have a Nature?* Milwaukee: Marquette University Press, 1980.

————. "Necessary Being." In *The Analytic Theist: An Alvin Plantinga Reader,* edited by James F. Sennett. Grand Rapids: Eerdmans, 1998, 214-224.

Pruss, Alexander R. "On Two Problems of Divine Simplicity." In *Oxford Studies in Philosophy of*

Religion, Vol. 1, edited by Jonathan L. Kvanvig. Oxford: Oxford University Press 2008, 150-167.

Richards, Jay Wesley. "Divine Simplicity: the Good, the Bad, and the Ugly." In *For Faith and Clarity: Philosophical Contributions to Christian Theology*, edited by James K. Beilby. Grand Rapids: Baker Academic, 2006, 157-178.

————. *The Untamed God: A Philosophical Exploration of Divine Perfection, Immutability, and Simplicity*. Downers Grove, Ill.: InterVarsity Press, 2003.

Rogers, Katherin A. "God, Time and Freedom." In *Philosophy of Religion: Classical and Contemporary Issues*, edited by Paul Copan and Chad V. Meister. Malden, MA: Blackwell Pub, 2008, 202-214.

Rowe, William L. "Divine Power, Goodness, and Knowledge." In *The Oxford Handbook of Philosophy of Religion*, edited by William J. Wainwright. New York: Oxford University Press, 2005, 15-34.

Senor, Thomas D. "Defending Divine Freedom." In *Oxford Studies in Philosophy of Religion, Vol. 1*, edited by Jonathan L. Kvanvig. Oxford: Oxford University Press 2008, 168-195.

————. "The Real Presence of an Eternal God." In *Metaphysics and God: Essays in Honor of Eleonore Stump*, edited by Kevin Timpe. New York: Routledge, 2009, 39-59.

Sherry, Patrick. "Beauty." In *A Companion to Philosophy of Religion*, edited by Philip L. Quinn and Charles Taliaferro. Cambridge, Mass: Blackwell, 1999, 279-285.

Soskice, Janet Martin. "Calling God 'Father.'" In *The Kindness of God: Metaphor, Gender, and Religious Language* by Janet Martin Soskice. Oxford: Oxford University Press, 2007, 66-83.

Stump, Eleonore and Norman Kretzmann. "Absolute Simplicity." *Faith and Philosophy* 2 (1985), 353-382.

―――. "Aquinas's Account of Divine Simplicity." In *Theologie Negative*, edited by Marco M. Olivetti. Padova: CEDAM, 2002, 575-584.

―――. "Aquinas on Being, Goodness, and Divine Simplicity." In *Miscellanea Mediaevalia Band 30: Die Logik des Transzendentalen* (Festschrift für Jan A. Aertsen zum 65. Geburtstag), edited by Martin Pickavé. Berlin: De Gruyter, 212-225.

―――. and Norman Kretzmann. "Being and Goodness." In *Divine and Human Action: Essays in the Metaphysics of Theism,* edited by Thomas V. Morris. Ithaca: Cornell University Press, 1988, 281-312.

―――. and Norman Kretzmann. "Eternity." *Journal of Philosophy* 78 (1981), 429-458, and reprinted elsewhere.

―――. "Eternity and God's Knowledge: A Reply to Shanley", *The American Catholic Philosophical Quarterly* 72, no. 3 (Summer 1998), pp. 439-445.

―――. "Eternity, Simplicity, and Presence." In *The Science of Being as Being: Metaphysical Investigations*, edited by Gregory T. Doolan. Washington, DC: Catholic University of America Press, 2011, 243-263.

————. "God's Simplicity." In *The Oxford Handbook of Aquinas*, edited by Brian Davies and Eleonore Stump. Oxford: Oxford University Press, 2012, 135-146.

————. "Presence and Omnipresence." In *Liberal Faith: Essays in Honor of Philip Quinn*, edited Paul J. Weithman. Notre Dame, IN: University of Notre Dame Press, 2008), 59-82.

————. "Simplicity." In *A Companion to Philosophy of Religion,* edited by Philip L. Quinn and Charles Taliaferro. Cambridge, Mass: Blackwell, 1999, 250-256.

Swinburne, Richard. *The Coherence of Theism*. Oxford: Clarendon Press, 1977.

Taliaferro, Charles. "Divine Power." Chap. 3 in *Contemporary Philosophy of Religion,* by Charles Taliaferro. Malden: Blackwell, 1998, 61-74.

————. "Incorporeality." In *A Companion to Philosophy of Religion,* edited by Philip L. Quinn and Charles Taliaferro. Cambridge, Mass: Blackwell, 1999, 271-278.

Tanner, Kathryn E. "Theological Perspectives on God as an Invisible Force." In *Invisible Forces and Powerful Beliefs: Gravity, Gods, and Minds,* Chicago Social Brain Network. Upper Saddle River, N.J.: FT Press Science, 2011, 157-168.

————. "The Use of the Perceived Properties of Light as a Theological Analogy." In *Light from Light: Scientists and Theologians in Dialogue,* edited by Gerald O'Collins and Mary Ann Meyers. Grand

Rapids, Mich: W.B. Eerdmans Pub. Co, 2012, 122-130.

Urban, Linwood, and Douglas N. Walton, editors. *The Power of God: Readings on Omnipotence and Evil.* New York: Oxford University Press, 1978.

Wainwright, William J. "Omnipotence, Omniscience, and Omnipresence." In *The Cambridge Companion to Christian Philosophical Theology,* edited by Charles Taliaferro and Chad V. Meister. Cambridge: Cambridge University Press, 2010, 46-65.

Wierenga, Edward R. *The Nature of God: An Inquiry into Divine Attributes.* Ithaca: Cornell University Press, 1989.

————. "Omnipresence." In *A Companion to Philosophy of Religion,* edited by Philip L. Quinn and Charles Taliaferro. Cambridge, Mass: Blackwell, 1999, 286-290.

————. "Omniscience." In *The Oxford Handbook of Philosophical Theology,* edited by Thomas P. Flint and Michael C. Rea. Oxford: Oxford University Press, 2009, 129-144.

Williams, C. J. F. "Being." In *A Companion to Philosophy of Religion,* edited by Philip L. Quinn and Charles Taliaferro. Cambridge, Mass: Blackwell, 1999, 223-228.

Wolterstorff, Nicholas. "God is Everlasting." In *Philosophy of Religion: Selected Readings,* 2nd Edition. Edited by Michael L. Peterson, William Hasker, Bruce Reichenbach and David Basinger. New York: Oxford University Press, 2001, 139-148.

————. "Justice of God." In *For Faith and Clarity: Philosophical Contributions to Christian Theology,* edited by James K. Beilby. Grand Rapids: Baker Academic, 2006, 179-200.

Van Inwagen, Peter. "What Does an Omniscient Being Know about the Future." In *Oxford Studies in Philosophy of Religion, Vol. 1,* edited by Jonathan L. Kvanvig. Oxford: Oxford University Press 2008, 216-230.

Yandell, Keith. "Divine Necessity and Divine Goodness." In *Divine and Human Action: Essays in the Metaphysics of Theism,* edited by Thomas V. Morris. Ithaca: Cornell University Press, 1988, 313-344.

Zagzebski, Linda. "Omnisubjectivity." In *Oxford Studies in Philosophy of Religion, Vol. 1,* edited by Jonathan L. Kvanvig. Oxford: Oxford University Press 2008, 231-248.

Divine agency/action

Abraham, William J. "Miracles." In *An Introduction to the Philosophy of Religion,* by William J. Abraham. Englewood Cliffs: Prentice-Hall, 1985, 152-164.

Allen, Diogenes. "Faith and the Recognition of God's Activity." In *Divine Action: Studies Inspired by the Philosophical Theology of Austin Farrer,* edited by Brian Hebblethwaite and Edward Henderson. Edinburgh: T & T Clark, 1990, 197-210.

Alston, William P. "Divine and Human Action." In *Divine Nature and Human Language: Essays in Philosophical Theology,* by William P. Alston. Ithaca: Cornell University Press, 1989, 81-102.

———. "God's Action in the World." In *Divine Nature and Human Language: Essays in Philosophical Theology,* by William P. Alston. Ithaca: Cornell University Press, 1989, 197-222.

———. "How to Think about Divine Action." In *Divine Action: Studies Inspired by the Philosophical Theology of Austin Farrer,* edited by Brian Hebblethwaite and Edward Henderson. Edinburgh: T & T Clark, 1990, 51-70.

Brown, David. "God and Symbolic Action." In *Divine Action: Studies Inspired by the Philosophical Theology of Austin Farrer,* edited by Brian Hebblethwaite and Edward Henderson. Edinburgh: T & T Clark, 1990, 103-122.

Brümmer, Vincent. *Speaking of a Personal God: An Essay in Philosophical Theology.* Cambridge: Cambridge University Press, 1992.

Burrell, David. "Divine Practical Knowing: How an Eternal God Acts in Time." In *Divine Action: Studies Inspired by the Philosophical Theology of Austin Farrer,* edited by Brian Hebblethwaite and Edward Henderson. Edinburgh: T & T Clark, 1990, 93-102.

Coakley, Sarah. "Providence and the Evolutionary Phenomenon of 'Cooperation': A Systematic Proposal." In *The Providence of God: Deus Habet Consilium,* edited by Francesca Aran Murphy and

Philip G. Ziegler. Edinburgh, T&T Clark, 2009, 181–195.

Davison, Scott A. "Petitionary Prayer." In *The Oxford Handbook of Philosophical Theology*, edited by Thomas P. Flint and Michael C. Rea. Oxford: Oxford University Press, 2009, 286-305.

Draper, Paul. "God, Science, and Naturalism." In *The Oxford Handbook of Philosophy of Religion*, edited by William J. Wainwright. New York: Oxford University Press, 2005, 272-303.

Eaton, Jeffrey. "Divine Action and Human Liberation." In *Divine Action: Studies Inspired by the Philosophical Theology of Austin Farrer,* edited by Brian Hebblethwaite and Edward Henderson. Edinburgh: T & T Clark, 1990, 211-229

Flint. Thomas P. "Fittingness and Divine Action in Cur Deus Homo." In *Metaphysics and God: Essays in Honor of Eleonore Stump,* edited by Kevin Timpe. New York: Routledge, 2009, 97-111.

Forsman, Rodger. "'Double Agency' and Identifying Reference to God." In *Divine Action: Studies Inspired by the Philosophical Theology of Austin Farrer,* edited by Brian Hebblethwaite and Edward Henderson. Edinburgh: T & T Clark, 1990, 123-142.

Geach, P. T. "Praying for Things to Happen." In *God and the Soul* by P. T. Geach. London: Routledge & K. Paul, 1969, 86-99.

Harris, Harriet. "Prayer." In *The Cambridge Companion to Christian Philosophical Theology,* edited by

Charles Taliaferro and Chad V. Meister. Cambridge: Cambridge University Press, 2010, 216-237.

Holtzer, Steven W. "The Possibility of Incorporeal Agency." In *The Rationality of Religious Belief: Essays in Honour of Basil Mitchell*, edited by William J. Abraham and Steven W. Holtzer. Oxford: Oxford University Press, 1987, 189-210.

Mavrodes, George I. "Miracles." In *The Oxford Handbook of Philosophy of Religion*, edited by William J. Wainwright. New York: Oxford University Press, 2005, 304-321.

McClain, F. Michael. "Narrative Interpretation and the Problem of Double Agency." In *Divine Action: Studies Inspired by the Philosophical Theology of Austin Farrer,* edited by Brian Hebblethwaite and Edward Henderson. Edinburgh: T & T Clark, 1990, 143-172.

Moser, Paul K. "Christianity and Miracles," forthcoming in *Debating Christian Theism*, edited by Chad Meister, J.P. Moreland, and K. Sweis. Oxford University Press, 2012.

Plantinga. Alvin. "Can God Break the Laws?" In *God and the Ethics of Belief: New Essays in Philosophy of Religion,* edited by Andrew Dole and Andrew Chignell. New York: Cambridge University Press, 2005, 31-58.

Price, H. H. "Petitionary Prayer and Telepathy." In *Essays in the Philosophy of Religion: Based on the Sarum Lectures, 1971* by H. H. Price. Oxford: Clarendon Press, 1972.

Russell, Robert John. "Quantum Physics and the Theology of Non-Interventionist Objective Divine Action." In *The Oxford Handbook of Religion and Science* edited by Philip Clayton and Zachary Simpson. Oxford: Oxford University Press, 2006, 579-595.

Schlesinger, George. "Miracles." In *A Companion to Philosophy of Religion*, edited by Philip L. Quinn and Charles Taliaferro. Cambridge, Mass: Blackwell Publishers, 1997, 360-366.

Stump, Eleonore. "God's Obligations." *Philosophical Perspectives,* 6, edited by James Tomberlin. Atascadero, CA: Ridgeview Publishing, (1992), 475-492.

―――. "Petitionary Prayer." In *A Companion to Philosophy of Religion,* edited by Philip L. Quinn and Charles Taliaferro. Cambridge, Mass: Blackwell, 1999, 577-583.

――― and Norman Kretzmann. "Eternity, Awareness, and Action." *Faith and Philosophy*, 9 (1992), 463-482.

――― and Norman Kretzmann. "God's Knowledge and Its Causal Efficacy." In *The Rationality of Belief and the Plurality of Faith: Essays in Honor of William P. Alston,* edited by Thomas D. Senor. Ithaca: Cornell University Press, 1995., 94-124.

Sullivan, Thomas D. and Sandra Menssen. "Revelation and Miracles." In *The Cambridge Companion to Christian Philosophical Theology,* edited by Charles Taliaferro and Chad V. Meister. Cambridge:

Cambridge University Press, 2010, 201-215.

Teselle, Eugene. "Divine Action: The Doctrinal Tradition." In *Divine Action: Studies Inspired by the Philosophical Theology of Austin Farrer,* edited by Brian Hebblethwaite and Edward Henderson. Edinburgh: T & T Clark, 1990, 71-92.

Thomas, Owen C. "Recent Thought on Divine Agency." In *Divine Action: Studies Inspired by the Philosophical Theology of Austin Farrer,* edited by Brian Hebblethwaite and Edward Henderson. Edinburgh: T & T Clark, 1990, 35-50.

Tracy, Thomas F.. "Divine Action." In *A Companion to Philosophy of Religion,* edited by Philip L. Quinn and Charles Taliaferro. Cambridge, Mass: Blackwell, 1999, 299-305.

———. "Narrative Theology and the Acts of God." In *Divine Action: Studies Inspired by the Philosophical Theology of Austin Farrer,* edited by Brian Hebblethwaite and Edward Henderson. Edinburgh: T & T Clark, 1990, 173-196.

———. "Theologies of Divine Action." In *The Oxford Handbook of Religion and Science* edited by Philip Clayton and Zachary Simpson. Oxford: Oxford University Press, 2006, 596-611.

3

Creation

*Creation, Providence (law, miracle), Predestination,
Evil, Anthropology, Imago Dei, Sin*

Creation

Adams, Robert. "Must God Create the Best?" In *The
Virtue of Faith and Other Essays in Philosophical
Theology,* by Robert Adams. New York: Oxford
University Press, 1987, 51-64.

Austin, Eric E. "Quentin Smith on the Logical
Impossibility of a Divine Cause." In *Philosophia
Christi,* edited by Craig J. Hazen. Series 2, vol. 3,
number 2 (2001), 525-531.

Collins, Robin. "Divine Action and Evolution." In *The
Oxford Handbook of Philosophical Theology,* edited
by Thomas P. Flint and Michael C. Rea. Oxford:
Oxford University Press, 2009, 241-260.

Craig, William Lane. "Theism and physical cosmology."
In *A Companion to Philosophy of Religion,* edited by
Philip L. Quinn and Charles Taliaferro. Cambridge,
Mass: Blackwell, 1999, 419-425.

Ferguson, David. "Creation." In *The Oxford Handbook of Systematic Theology,* edited by J. B. Webster, Kathryn Tanner, and Iain R. Torrance. Oxford: Oxford University Press, 2007, 72-90.

Fischer, John Martin. "More on Molinism." In *Metaphysics and God: Essays in Honor of Eleonore Stump,* edited by Kevin Timpe. New York: Routledge, 2009, 127-144.

Flew, Antony and MacKinnon, D. M. "Creation." In *New Essays in Philosophical Theology,* edited by Antony Flew and Alasdair MacIntyre. London: SCM Press, 1955, 170-186.

Freddoso, Alfred J. "Medieval Aristotelianism and the Case Against Secondary Causation in Nature." In *Divine and Human Action: Essays in the Metaphysics of Theism,* edited by Thomas V. Morris. Ithaca: Cornell University Press, 1988, 74-118.

Geach, P. T. "Causality and Creation." In *God and the Soul* by P. T. Geach. New York: Schocken Books, 1969.

Gunton, Colin. "The Doctrine of Creation." In *The Cambridge Companion to Christian Doctrine,* edited by Colin E. Gunton. Cambridge: Cambridge University Press, 1997, 141-157.

Hasker, William. "Theism and Evolutionary Biology." In *A Companion to Philosophy of Religion,* edited by Philip L. Quinn and Charles Taliaferro. Cambridge, Mass: Blackwell, 1999, 426-433.

Helm, Paul. "Time and Creation in Augustine's *Confessions.*" In *Faith and Understanding* by Paul

Helm. Grand Rapids, Mich: Wm. B. Eerdmans Pub, 1997.

Kvanvig, Jonathan L. "Conservation, Concurrence, and Counterfactuals of Freedom." In *Metaphysics and God: Essays in Honor of Eleonore Stump*, edited by Kevin Timpe. New York: Routledge, 2009, 112-126.

———— and Hugh J. McCann. "Divine Conservation and the Persistence of the World." In *Divine and Human Action: Essays in the Metaphysics of Theism,* edited by Thomas V. Morris. Ithaca: Cornell University Press, 1988, 13-49.

Mann, William E. "Divine Sovereignty and Aseity." In *The Oxford Handbook of Philosophy of Religion*, edited by William J. Wainwright. New York: Oxford University Press, 2005, 35-58.

Marshall, Bruce D. "Are there Angels?" In *Why Are We Here?: Everyday Questions and the Christian Life*, edited by Ronald F. Thiemann & William C. Placher. Harrisburg, PA: Trinity Press International, 1998, 69-83.

McCann, Hugh J. "Creation and Conservation." In *A Companion to Philosophy of Religion,* edited by Philip L. Quinn and Charles Taliaferro. Cambridge, Mass: Blackwell, 1999, 306-312.

Murray, Michael J. "Science and Religion in Constructive Engagement." In *Analytic Theology: New Essays in the Philosophy of Theology*, edited by Oliver D. Crisp and Michael C. Rea. Oxford: Oxford University Press, 2009, 233-250.

O'Connor, Timothy. "Theism and the Scope of Contingency." In *Oxford Studies in Philosophy of Religion, Vol. 1*, edited by Jonathan L. Kvanvig. Oxford: Oxford University Press 2008, 134-149.

Plantinga, Alvin. "Evolution and Design." In *For Faith and Clarity: Philosophical Contributions to Christian Theology,* edited by James K. Beilby. Grand Rapids: Baker Academic, 2006, 201-218.

Quinn, Philip L. "Divine Conservation, Continuous Creation, and Human Action." In *The Existence and Nature of God,* edited by Alfred J. Freddoso. Notre Dame: University of Notre Dame Press, 1983, 55-79.

———. "Divine Conservation, Secondary Causes, and Occasionalism." In *Divine and Human Action: Essays in the Metaphysics of Theism,* edited by Thomas V. Morris. Ithaca: Cornell University Press, 1988, 74-118.

Taliaferro, Charles. "Divine Intelligence and the Structure of the Cosmos." In *Contemporary Philosophy of Religion,* by Charles Taliaferro. Malden, Mass: Blackwell, 1997, 106-142.

———. "Theism and Naturalism." In *Contemporary Philosophy of Religion,* by Charles Taliaferro. Malden, Mass: Blackwell, 1997, 350-393.

Tanner, Kathryn E. "Creation and Providence" in *The Cambridge Companion to Karl Barth,* edited by J. B. Webster. Cambridge, U.K.: Cambridge University Press, 2000, 111-126.

———. "Creation in the *Summa Theologiae*" In *The Cambridge Companion to the Summa Theologiae,* edited by Philip McCosker and Denys Turner. Cambridge: Cambridge University Press, forthcoming 2013.

———. "Is God in Charge?: Creation and Providence." In *Essentials of Christian Theology,* edited by Stanley J. Grenz and William C. Placher. Louisville: Westminster John Knox Press, 2003, 116-131.

Van Inwagen, Peter. "God and Other Uncreated Things." In *Metaphysics and God: Essays in Honor of Eleonore Stump,* edited by Kevin Timpe. New York: Routledge, 2009, 3-20.

———. "The Place of Chance in a World Sustained by God." In *Oxford Readings in Philosophical Theology Vol. 2, Providence, Scripture, and Resurrection,* edited by Michael C. Rea. Oxford: Oxford University Press, 2009, 104-126.

Zagzebski, Linda. "Individual Essence and the Creation." In *Divine and Human Action: Essays in the Metaphysics of Theism,* edited by Thomas V. Morris. Ithaca: Cornell University Press, 1988, 19-147.

Providence

Davison, Scott A. "Divine Providence and Human Freedom." In *Reason for the Hope Within,* edited by Michael J. Murray. Grand Rapids: Eerdmans, 1999, 217-238.

Deerborn, Derk. "Free Will, Evil, and Divine Providence." In *God and the Ethics of Belief: New*

Essays in Philosophy of Religion, edited by Andrew Dole and Andrew Chignell. New York: Cambridge University Press, 2005, 77-98.

Fischer, John Martin. "Freedom and Actuality." In *Divine and Human Action: Essays in the Metaphysics of Theism,* edited by Thomas V. Morris. Ithaca: Cornell University Press, 1988, 236-256.

Flint, Thomas P. *Divine Providence: The Molinist Account.* Ithaca, N.Y.: Cornell University Press, 1998.

————. "Divine Providence." In *The Oxford Handbook of Philosophical Theology,* edited by Thomas P. Flint and Michael C. Rea. Oxford: Oxford University Press, 2009, 262-285.

————. "Two Accounts of Providence." In *Oxford Readings in Philosophical Theology Vol. 2, Providence, Scripture, and Resurrection,* edited by Michael C. Rea. Oxford: Oxford University Press, 2009, 17-44.

Hasker, William. "Eternity and Providence." In *The Cambridge Companion to Christian Philosophical Theology,* edited by Charles Taliaferro and Chad V. Meister. Cambridge: Cambridge University Press, 2010, 81-94.

Hunt, David P. "Divine Providence and Simple Foreknowledge." In *Oxford Readings in Philosophical Theology Vol. 2, Providence, Scripture, and Resurrection,* edited by Michael C. Rea. Oxford: Oxford University Press, 2009, 84-103.

Issler, Klaus. "Divine Providence and Impetratory Prayer: A Review of Issues from Terrance Tiessen's *Providence and Prayer.*" In *Philosophia Christi* 3, edited by Craig J. Hazen. No. 2 (2001), 533-541.

Lucas, J. R. "Providence." In *Freedom and Grace,* by J. R. Lucas. London: SPCK, 1976, 27-34.

Mann, William E. "God's Freedom, Human Freedom, and God's Responsibility for Sin." In *Divine and Human Action: Essays in the Metaphysics of Theism,* edited by Thomas V. Morris. Ithaca: Cornell University Press, 1988, 182-210.

Tanner, Kathryn E. "Creation and Providence" in *The Cambridge Companion to Karl Barth,* edited by J. B. Webster. Cambridge, U.K.: Cambridge University Press, 2000, 111-126.

―――. "Is God in Charge?: Creation and Providence." In *Essentials of Christian Theology,* edited by Stanley J. Grenz and William C. Placher. Louisville: Westminster John Knox Press, 2003, 116-131.

Wierenga, Edward. "Providence, Middle Knowledge, and the Grounding Objection." In *Philosophia Christi* 3, edited by Craig J. Hazen. No. 2 (2001), 447-454.

Wood, Charles Monroe. *The Question of Providence.* Louisville, Ky: Westminster John Knox Press, 2008.

―――. "Providence." In *The Oxford Handbook of Systematic Theology,* edited by J. B. Webster, Kathryn Tanner, and Iain R. Torrance. Oxford: Oxford University Press, 2007, 91-104.

Predestination

Beilby, James K. and Paul R. Eddy editors. *Divine Foreknowledge: Four Views.* Downers Grove: InterVarsity Press, 2001.

Flint, Thomas P. "Providence and Predestination." In *A Companion to Philosophy of Religion,* edited by Philip L. Quinn and Charles Taliaferro. Cambridge, Mass: Blackwell Publishers, 1999, 569-576.

Plantinga, Alvin. "On Ockham's Way Out." In *The Analytic Theist: An Alvin Plantinga Reader,* edited by James F. Sennett. Grand Rapids: Eerdmans, 1998, 258-292.

Sonderegger, Katherine. "Election." In *The Oxford Handbook of Systematic Theology,* edited by J. B. Webster, Kathryn Tanner, and Iain R. Torrance. Oxford: Oxford University Press, 2007, 105-120.

Zagzebski, Linda Trinkaus. *The Dilemma of Freedom and Foreknowledge.* New York: Oxford University Press, 1991.

Evil

Adams, Marilyn McCord. *Christ and Horrors: The Coherence of Christology.* Cambridge: Cambridge University Press, 2006.

Draper, Paul. "More Pain and Pleasure: A Reply to Otte." In *Christian Faith and the Problem of Evil,* edited by Peter Van Inwagen. Grand Rapids: W B. Eerdmans,

2004, 41-54.

Mesiter, Chad. "The Problem of Evil." In *The Cambridge Companion to Christian Philosophical Theology*, edited by Charles Taliaferro and Chad V. Meister. Cambridge: Cambridge University Press, 2010, 152-169.

Otte, Richard. "Probability and Draper's Evidential Argument from Evil." In *Christian Faith and the Problem of Evil*, edited by Peter Van Inwagen. Grand Rapids: W B. Eerdmans, 2004, 26-40.

Plantinga, Alvin. *God, Freedom, and Evil*. Grand Rapids: Eerdmans, 1977.

Stump, Eleonore. "Narrative and the Problem of Evil: Suffering and Redemption." In *The Redemption: An Interdisciplinary Symposium on Christ As Redeemer*, edited by Stephen T. Davis, Daniel Kendall and Gerald O'Collins. Oxford: Oxford University Press, 2004, 207-234.

———. "The Problem of Evil." In *Faith and Philosophy* 2, no. 4 (October 1985), 392-423.

———. "The Problem of Evil: Analytic Philosophy and Narrative." In *Analytic Theology: New Essays in the Philosophy of Theology*, edited by Oliver D. Crisp and Michael C. Rea. Oxford: Oxford University Press, 2009, 251-264.

———. "The Problem of Evil and the Desires of the Heart." In *Oxford Studies in Philosophy of Religion, Vol. 1*, edited by Jonathan L. Kvanvig. Oxford: Oxford University Press 2008, 196-215.

————. "The Problem of Evil and the History of Peoples: 'Think Amalek.'" In *Divine Evil?: The Moral Character of the God of Abraham*, edited by Michael Bergmann, Michael J. Murray and Michael C. Rea. Oxford: New York, 2011, 179-197.

————. "The Problem of Suffering (2008)." In *Thomas Aquinas: Teacher and Scholar: the Aquinas Lectures at Maynooth, Volume 2: 2002-2010*, edited by J. J. McEvoy, Michael Dunne and Julia Hynes. Dublin: Four Courts Press, 2012, 101-119.

————. "Providence and the Problem of Evil." In *Christian Philosophy*, edited by Thomas P. Flint. Notre Dame: University of Notre Dame Press, 1990, 51-91.

————. "Reply to Draper." In *Divine Evil?: The Moral Character of the God of Abraham*, edited by Michael Bergmann, Michael J. Murray and Michael C. Rea. Oxford: New York, 2011, 204-208.

————. "Saadia Gaon on the Problem of Evil", *Faith and Philosophy* 14 (October 1997), 523-549.

————. "Samson and Self-Destroying Evil." In *Philosophers and the Jewish Bible*, edited by Charles Harry Manekin and Robert Eisen. Bethesda, Md: University Press of Maryland, 2008, 199-217.

————. "Second Person Accounts and the Problem of Evil" in *Perspectives in Contemporary Philosophy of Religion*, Schriften der Luther-Agricola-Gesellschaft 46, edited by Timo Koistinen and Tommi Lehtonen, (Helsinki: Luther-Agricola-Society, 2000), 88-113.

————. *Wandering in Darkness, Narrative and the*

Problem of Suffering. Oxford; Clarendon Press, 2010.

Van Inwagen, Peter. "The Argument from Evil." In *Christian Faith and the Problem of Evil,* edited by Peter Van Inwagen. Grand Rapids: W B. Eerdmans, 2004, 55-73.

Anthropology

Audi, Robert. "Theism and the Scientific Understanding of the Mind." In *A Companion to Philosophy of Religion*, edited by Philip L. Quinn and Charles Taliaferro. Cambridge, Mass: Blackwell Publishers, 1999, 433-441.

Baker, Lynne Rudder. "Need a Christian be a Mind/Body Dualist?" In *Oxford Readings in Philosophical Theology Vol. 2, Providence, Scripture, and Resurrection*, edited by Michael C. Rea. Oxford: Oxford University Press, 2009, 347-363.

————. "Persons and the Natural Order." In *Persons: Human and Divine,* edited by Peter Van Inwagen and Dean W. Zimmerman. Oxford: Clarendon, 2007, 261-278.

————. "Unity without Identity: A New Look at Material Constitution." In *Midwest Studies in Philosophy* 23 (1999):144-165.

Binde, Per. "Nature in Roman Catholic Tradition." *Anthropological Quarterly* 74, no. 1 (2001), 15-27.

Cavadini, John C. "Feeling Right: Augustine on the Passions and Sexual Desire." *Augustinian Studies,* 36, no. 1 (2005).

Centore, F. F. *Persons, a Comparative Account of the Six Possible Theories.* Westport, Conn: Greenwood Press, 1979.

Coakley, Sarah. "Creaturehood before God, Male and Female", *Theology* 93, 1990, (reprinted in *Readings in Modern Theology*, edited Robin Gill. London: S.P.C.K., 1995, 343–353.

————. "Visions of the Self in Late Medieval Christianity: Some Cross-Disciplinary Reflections." In *Philosophy, Religion and the Spiritual Life*, edited by Michael McGhee. Royal Institute of Philosophy Supplements. Cambridge: Cambridge University Press, 1992, 89–103.

Cooper, John W. *Body, Soul, and Life Everlasting, Biblical Anthropology and the Monism-Dualism and Debate*. Grand Rapids, Mich.: Eerdmans, 1989.

Donagan, Alan. "Human Ends and Human Actions: An Exploration in St. Thomas's Treatment." In *Reflections on Philosophy and Religion*, by Alan Donagan, edited by Anthony N. Perovich. New York: Oxford University Press, 1999, 81-98.

————. "St. Thomas Aquinas on the Analysis of Human Action." In *Reflections on Philosophy and Religion*, by Alan Donagan, edited by Anthony N. Perovich. New York: Oxford University Press, 1999, 67-80.

Evans, Stephen C. "Healing Old Wounds and Recovering Old Insights: Towards a Christian View of the Person for Today." In *Christian Theology in the Modern World: Faith and Practice from an Evangelical Point of View*, edited by Mark Noll and David Wells. Eerdmans, 1988, 68-86.

————. "Human Persons as Substantial Achievers." *Philosophia Reformata* 58 (1993), 100-112.

―――. "Separable Souls: A Defense of Minimal Dualism." *Southern Journal of Philosophy,* XIX, no. 3, 313-331.

―――. "Separable Souls: Dualism, Selfhood, and the Possibility of Life After Death." *The Christian Scholar's Review,* XXXIV, no. 3 (Spring 2005), 327-340.

―――. "The Social Character of the Self: Psychological and Theological Perspectives." In *Judeo-Christian Perspectives on Psychology: Human Nature, Motivation and Change,* edited by William R. Miller and Harold D. Delaney. Washington, D.C.: American Psychological Association Publications, 2005, 73-93.

―――. "Where There's a Will, There's a Way: Kierkegaard's Theory of Action." In *Writing the Politics of Difference,* edited by Hugh J. Silverman. SUNY Press, 1991, 73-88.

Geach, P. T. *God and the Soul.* London: Routledge & K. Paul, 1969.

Griffiths, Paul J. "Metaphysics and Personality Theory." In *Limning the Psyche: Explorations in Christian Psychology,* edited by Robert C. Roberts and Mark R. Talbot. Grand Rapids, Michigan: Eerdmans, 1997, 41-57.

Harré, Rom. "Body and Soul: Physical Properties and Cartesian Mind." In *Reason and the Christian Religion: Essays in Honour of Richard Swinburne,* edited by Alan G. Padgett. Oxford: Clarendon Press, 1994, 303-328.

Hasker, William. "Philosophical Contributions to Theological Anthropology." In *For Faith and Clarity: Philosophical Contributions to Christian Theology,* edited by James K. Beilby. Grand Rapids: Baker Academic, 2006, 243-260.

Hudson, Hud. "I am Not an Animal!" In *Persons: Human and Divine,* edited by Peter Van Inwagen and Dean W. Zimmerman. Oxford: Clarendon, 2007, 216-236.

Kelsey, David H. "The Human Creature." In *The Oxford Handbook of Systematic Theology,* edited by J. B. Webster, Kathryn Tanner, and Iain R. Torrance. Oxford: Oxford University Press, 2007, 121-139.

Kelsey, David H. *Eccentric Existence: A Theological Anthropology* (2-Volume Set. Louisville, Ky: Westminster John Knox Press, 2009.

LaRock, Eric F. "Dualistic Interaction, Neural Dependence, and Aquinas's Composite View." In *Philosophia Christi*, edited by Craig J. Hazen. Series 2, vol. 3, no 2 (2001), 459-472.

Lucas. J. R. "The Soul." In *Faith and Logic: Oxford Essays in Philosophical Theology* edited by Basil Mitchell. London: Allen & Unwin, 1958, 132-148.

McFadyen, Alistair I. *The Call to Personhood: A Christian Theory of the Individual in Social Relationships.* Cambridge: Cambridge University Press, 1990.

Mitchell, Basil. "Man – A Reasonable Being." In *How to Play Theological Ping-Pong: And Other Essays on Faith and Reason,* by Basil Mitchell, edited by

William J. Abraham, and Robert Prevost. London: Hodder and Stoughton, 1990, 198-211.

Moreland, James Porter, and Scott B. Rae. *Body & Soul: Human Nature & the Crisis in Ethics.* Downers Grove, Ill: InterVarsity Press, 2000. (Part 1: Metaphysical reflections on human personhood; Part 2: Ethical reflections on human personhood).

Moser, Paul K. "The Human Personal Factor as Moral Agency: Philosophical Foundations," in *The Review of Human Factor Studies,* Vol. 5, no.1 (2000), 33-42.

―――. "Human Persons: Their Nature, Faith, and Function." *Ex Auditu*, 13 (1997), 17-36.

――― and Arnold vander Nat. "Surviving Souls." *The Canadian Journal of Philosophy*, 23 (1993), 101-106.

Pasnau, Robert. *Thomas Aquinas on Human Nature: A Philosophical Study of Summa Theologiae 1a, 75-89.* Cambridge: Cambridge University Press, 2002.

Pilsner, Joseph. *The Specification of Human Actions in St. Thomas Aquinas.* Oxford: Oxford University Press, 2006.

Plantinga, Alvin. "Against Materialism." In *Oxford Readings in Philosophical Theology Vol. 2, Providence, Scripture, and Resurrection,* edited by Michael C. Rea. Oxford: Oxford University Press, 2009, 386-416.

Plantinga, Alvin. "Materialism and Christian Belief." In *Persons: Human and Divine,* edited by Peter Van Inwagen and Dean W. Zimmerman. Oxford: Clarendon, 2007, 99-141.

Quinn, Philip L. "On the Intrinsic Value of Human Persons." In *Persons: Human and Divine,* edited by Peter Van Inwagen and Dean W. Zimmerman. Oxford: Clarendon, 2007, 237-260.

Saarinen, Risto. "The Trinity, Creation, and Christian Anthropology." In *The Oxford Handbook of the Trinity,* edited by Gilles Emery and Matthew Levering. Oxford: Oxford University Press, 2011, 414-427.

Stump, Eleonore. "Intellect, Will, and the Principle of Alternate Possibilities." In *Perspectives on Moral Responsibility* edited by John Martin Fischer and Mark Ravizza. Ithaca, NY: Cornell University Press, 1993, 237-262.

Swinburne, Richard. "From Mental/Physical Identity to Substance Dualism." In *Persons: Human and Divine,* edited by Peter Van Inwagen and Dean W. Zimmerman. Oxford: Clarendon, 2007, 142-165.

Taliaferro, Charles. "Materialism, Positivism, and God." In *Contemporary Philosophy of Religion,* by Charles Taliaferro. Malden: Blackwell, 1998, 83-105.

————. "Philosophy of Mind and the Christian." In *Christian Theism and the Problems of Philosophy,* edited by Michael D. Beaty. Notre Dame: University of Notre Dame Press, 1990.

Tanner, Kathryn E. "The Difference Theological Anthropology Makes." In *Theology Today* 50 (1994), 567-579.

————. "Theological Anthropology." In *Anglican Systematic Theology Reader,* edited by Ralph

McMichael. SCM forthcoming 2012.

Van Inwagen, Peter. "Dualism and Materialism: Athens and Jerusalem?" In *The Possibility of Resurrection and Other Essays in Christian Apologetics,* by Peter Van Inwagen. Boulder, Colo: Westview Press, 1998, 53-68.

————. "A Materialist Ontology of the Human Person." In *Persons: Human and Divine,* edited by Peter Van Inwagen and Dean W. Zimmerman. Oxford: Clarendon, 2007, 199-215.

VanHoozer, Kevin. "Human Being, individual and social." In *The Cambridge Companion to Christian Doctrine,* edited by Colin E. Gunton. Cambridge: Cambridge University Press, 1997, 158-188.

Ward, Keith. *Defending the Soul.* Oxford: One World, 1992.

Zimmerman, Dean W. "The Compatibility of Materialism and Survival: The 'Falling Elevator' Model." In *Oxford Readings in Philosophical Theology Vol. 2, Providence, Scripture, and Resurrection*, edited by Michael C. Rea. Oxford: Oxford University Press, 2009, 328-346.

Imago Dei

Altmann, Alexander. "*Homo Imago Dei* in Jewish and Christian Theology." *The Journal of Religion* 48 (1968), 235-59.

Kaufman, Gordon D. "The *Imago Dei* as Man's

Historicity." *Journal of Religion* 36 (1956), 157-68.

Power, W. L. "Imago Dei—Imitatio Dei." *International Journal of Philosophy of Religion* 42 (1997), 131-141.

Soskice, Janet Martin. "Imago Dei." In *The Kindness of God: Metaphor, Gender, and Religious Language* by Janet Martin Soskice. Oxford: Oxford University Press, 2007, 35-51.

Tanner, Kathryn E. "In the Image of the Invisible" in *Apophatic Bodies: Negative Theology, Incarnation, and Relationality,* edited by Chris Boesel and Catherine Keller. New York: Fordham University Press, 2010, 117-136.

Sin

Adams, Robert Merrihew. "Involuntary Sins." *The Philosophical Review* 94 (1985), 3-31.

Cone, Orello. "The Pauline Doctrine of Sin." *The American Journal of Theology* 2 (1898), 241-267.

Crisp, Oliver D. "Original Sin and Atonement." In *The Oxford Handbook of Philosophical Theology,* edited by Thomas P. Flint and Michael C. Rea. Oxford: Oxford University Press, 2009, 430-451.

Geach, Peter. "Original Sin." In *Providence and Evil,* by Peter Geach. Cambridge: Cambridge University Press, 1977, 84-101.

Goldstein, Valerie Saiving. "The Human Situation: A Feminine View." *Journal of Religion* 40 (1960).

Hart, Trevor. "Redemption and Fall." In *The Cambridge Companion to Christian Doctrine,* edited by Colin E. Gunton. Cambridge: Cambridge University Press, 1997, 189-206.

Helm, Paul. "Jonathan Edwards on Original Sin." In *Faith and Understanding,* by Paul Helm. Grand Rapids, Mich: Wm. B. Eerdmans Pub, 1997.

Lossky, Vladimir. "Original Sin." In *Orthodox Theology: An Introduction,* by Vladimir Lossky. Crestwood, NY: St. Vladimir's Seminary Press, 1978, 79-94.

Lucas. J. R.. "The Origin of Sin." In *Freedom and Grace,* by J. R. Lucas. London: SPCK, 1976, 42-49.

McCord Adams, Marilyn. "Sin as Uncleanness." *Philosophical Perspectives*, 5, Philosophy of Religion, 1991, 1-28.

McFarland, Ian. "The Fall and Sin." In *The Oxford Handbook of Systematic Theology,* edited by J. B. Webster, Kathryn Tanner, and Iain R. Torrance. Oxford: Oxford University Press, 2007, 140-159.

Miller, J. Maxwell. "In the "Image" and "Likeness" of God." *Journal of Biblical Literature* 91 (1972), 289-304.

Oakes, Edward T. "Original Sin: A Disputation." *First Things*. November 1998, 16-24.

Plantinga, Alvin. "Sin and its Cognitive Consequences." In *Warranted Christian Belief,* by Alvin Plantinga. New York: Oxford University Press, 2000, 199-240.

Quinn, Philip L. "Sin and Original Sin." In *A Companion to Philosophy of Religion*, edited by Philip L. Quinn and Charles Taliaferro. Cambridge, Mass: Blackwell Publishers, 1999, 541-548.

Rea, Michael C. "The Metaphysics of Original Sin." In *Persons: Human and Divine,* edited by Peter Van Inwagen and Dean W. Zimmerman. Oxford: Clarendon, 2007, 319-356.

Tanner, Kathryn E. "Human Freedom, Human Sin, and God the Creator." In *The God Who Acts: Philosophical and Theological Explorations,* edited by Thomas F. Tracy. University Park, Pa: Pennsylvania State University Press, 1994, 111-136.

4

Christology

Person and Work of Christ

Person of Christ

Adams, Marilyn McCord. "Chalcedonian Chrsitology: A Christian Solution to the Problem of Evil." In *Philosophy and Theological Discourse*, edited by Stephen T. Davis. New York: St. Martin's Press, 1997, 173-198.

―――. "Christ as God-Man, Metaphysically Construed." In *Oxford Readings in Philosophical Theology, Vol. 1, Trinity, Incarnation, and Atonement*, edited by Michael C. Rea. Oxford: Oxford University Press, 2009, 239-266.

―――. *What Sort of Human Nature? : Medieval Philosophy and the Systematics of Christology*. Milwaukee: Marquette University Press, 1999.

Brown, David. "'Necessary' and 'Fitting' Reasons in Christian Theology." In *The Rationality of Religious Belief: Essays in Honour of Basil Mitchell*, edited by William J. Abraham and Steven W. Holtzer. Oxford: Oxford University Press, 1987, 211-230.

Coakley, Sarah. "The Identity of the Risen Jesus: Finding Jesus Christ in the Poor." In *Seeking the Identity of Jesus: A Pilgrimage,* edited by Beverly Roberts Gaventa and Richard B. Hays. Grand Rapids, MI: Eerdmans, 2008, 301–19, (reprinted with minor alterations in *'Godhead Here in Hiding': Incarnation and the History of Human Suffering,* edited by Terrence Merrigan and Frederik Glorieux. Leiden: Peeters, 2011, 309–27.

———. "The Resurrection and the 'Spiritual Senses': On Wittgenstein, Epistemology and the Risen Christ." In *Powers and Submissions: Spirituality, Philosophy, and Gender.* Oxford: Blackwell Publishers, 2002, 130-152.

———. "What Does Chalcedon Solve and What Does it Not? Some Reflections on the Status and Meaning of the Chalcedonian 'Definition.'" In *The Incarnation: An Interdisciplinary Symposium on the Incarnation of the Son of God,* edited by Stephen T. Davis, Daniel Kendall, and Gerald O'Collins. Oxford: Oxford University Press, 2002, 143-163.

Crisp, Oliver D. "Incarnation." In *The Oxford Handbook of Systematic Theology,* edited by J. B. Webster, Kathryn Tanner, and Iain R. Torrance. Oxford: Oxford University Press, 2007, 160-176.

Cross, R. "Aquinas on Nature, Hypostasis, and the Metaphysics of the Incarnation." *Thomist* 60 (1996): 171-202.

———. "The Incarnation." In *The Oxford Handbook of Philosophical Theology,* edited by

Thomas P. Flint and Michael C. Rea. Oxford: Oxford University Press, 2009, 452-475.

_____. *The Metaphysics of the Incarnation: Thomas Aquinas to Duns Scotus*. Oxford: Oxford University Press, 2002.

Daley, Brian E. "Nature and 'Mode of Union': Late Patristic Models for the Personal Unity of Christ." *The Incarnation: An Interdisciplinary Symposium on the Incarnation of the Son of God,* edited by Stephen T. Davis, Daniel Kendall, and Gerald O'Collins. Oxford: Oxford University Press, 2002, 164-196.

_____. "Word, Soul, and Flesh: Origen and Augustine on the Person of Christ."*Augustinian Studies* 36, no.2 (2005), 299-326.

Davis, Stephen T. *Encountering Jesus: A Debate on Christology*. Atlanta: John Knox Press, 1988.

———. "Resurrection." In *The Cambridge Companion to Christian Philosophical Theology,* edited by Charles Taliaferro and Chad V. Meister. Cambridge: Cambridge University Press, 2010, 108-123.

———. "Was Jesus Mad, Bad, or God?" *The Incarnation: An Interdisciplinary Symposium on the Incarnation of the Son of God,* edited by Stephen T. Davis, Daniel Kendall, and Gerald O'Collins. Oxford: Oxford University Press, 2002, 221-245.

Evans, Craig. E. "Jesus Self-designation: 'The Son of Man'." In *Oxford Readings in Philosophical Theology: Vol. 1: Trinity, Incarnation, and Atonement*, edited by Michael C. Rea. Oxford: Oxford University Press, 2009, 151-165.

Evans, C. Stephen. *Exploring Kenotic Christology: The Self-Emptying of God.* Oxford: Oxford University Press, 2006.

Feenstra, Ronald J. "Incarnation." In *A Companion to Philosophy of Religion,* edited by Philip L. Quinn and Charles Taliaferro. Cambridge, Mass: Blackwell, 1999, 532-540.

Forrest, Peter. "The Incarnation: A Philosophical Case for Kenosis." In *Oxford Readings in Philosophical Theology: Vol. 1: Trinity, Incarnation, and Atonement,* edited by Michael C. Rea. Oxford: Oxford University Press, 2009, 225-238.

Griffiths, Paul J. "One Jesus, Many Christs?" *Pro Ecclesia* 7 (1998), 152-171.

Helm, Paul. "Anselm's Understanding of the Incarnation." In *Faith and Understanding,* by Paul Helm. Grand Rapids, Mich: Wm. B. Eerdmans Pub, 1997.

Howard-Snyder, Daniel. "Was Jesus Mad, Bad, or God?... or Merely Mistaken?" *Faith and Philosophy* 21, no. 4 (2004) 456-479.

Janzen, Grace. "Incarnation and Epistemology." *Theology* 83 (May 1983): 171.

Marshall, Bruce D. "Christologic: A Reply to Some Questions about Christology in Conflict" *Philosophy and Theology* 6, no. 2 (Winter 1991), 145-158.

———. "Christology," In *The Blackwell Encyclopedia of Modern Christian Thought,* edited by Alister E. McGrath. Oxford: Blackwell, 1993, 80-93.

Merricks, Trenton. "The Word Made Flesh: Dualism, Physicalism, and the Incarnation." In *Persons: Human and Divine,* edited by Peter Van Inwagen and Dean W. Zimmerman. Oxford: Clarendon, 2007, 281-300.

Morris, Thomas V. "Jesus Christ was Fully God and Fully Human." In *Philosophy of Religion: Selected Readings,* 2nd Edition. Edited by Michael L. Peterson, William Hasker, Bruce Reichenbach and David Basinger. New York: Oxford University Press, 2001, 599-607.

———. *The Logic of God Incarnate.* Eugene: Wipf & Stock Publishers, 2001.

———. "The Metaphysics of God Incarnate." In *Oxford Readings in Philosophical Theology: Vol. 1: Trinity, Incarnation, and Atonement,* edited by Michael C. Rea. Oxford: Oxford University Press, 2009, 211.224.

Owen, H.P. "The New Testament and the Incarnation: A Study in Doctrinal Development." Religious Studies 8 (1972), 221-232.

Rahner, Karl. "Christology Within an Evolutionary View of the World." In *Theological Investigations,* vol. 5. Translated by K. Kruger. New York: Crossroad, 1983.

Rogers, Katherin A. "Incarnation." In *The Cambridge Companion to Christian Philosophical Theology,* edited by Charles Taliaferro and Chad V. Meister. Cambridge: Cambridge University Press, 2010, 95-107.

Senor, T. "God, Supernatural Kinds, and the Incarnation." *Religious Studies* 27 (1991): 353-370.

―――. "Incarnation and the Trinity." In *Reason for the Hope Within,* edited by Michael J. Murray. Grand Rapids: Eerdmans, 1999, 238-260.

―――. "Incarnation and Timelessness." In *Faith and Philosophy* 7, no. 2 (1990) 149-164.

Stump, Eleonore. "Aquinas' Metaphysics of the Incarnation." In *Incarnation: An Interdisciplinary Symposium on the Incarnation of the Son of God.* Edited by Stephen T. Davis, Daniel Kendall, and Gerald O'Collins. Oxford: Oxford University Press, 2002, 197-220.

―――. "Review of *Logic of God Incarnate* by Thomas Morris." *Faith and Philosophy,* VI, no. 2, (April 1989): 218-223.

―――. "Word and Incarnation." In *Incarnation,* edited by M. Olivetti. Padua: Edam, 1999, 543-554.

Swinburne, Richard. "Could God Become Man?" In *The Philosophy in Christianity,* edited by Godfrey N. A. Vesey. Cambridge: Cambridge University Press, 1989.

Tanner, Kathryn. "Jesus Christ." In *The Cambridge Companion to Christian Doctrine,* edited by Colin E. Gunton. Cambridge: Cambridge University Press, 1997, 245-272.

Van Inwagen, Peter. "Incarnation and Christology." In *Routledge Encyclopedia of Philosophy,* edited by Craig Edward. New York: Routledge, 1999, 4: 725-732.

———. "Not by Confusion of Substance, but by Unity of Person." In *Reason and the Christian Religion: Essays in Honour of Richard Swinburne*, edited by Alan G. Padgett. Oxford: Clarendon Press, 1994, 201-226.

White, Vernon. *Atonement and Incarnation, an Essay in Universalism and Particularity.* Cambridge: Cambridge University Press, 1991.

Zagzebski, Linda. "The Incarnation and Virtue Ethics." " In *Incarnation: An Interdisciplinary Symposium on the Incarnation of the Son of God.* Ed. by Stephen T. Davis, Daniel Kendall, and Gerald O'Collins. Oxford: Oxford University Press, 2002, 313-331.

Work of Christ

Adams, Robert Mettihew. "Atoning Transactions." In *Philosophy and Theological Discourse*, edited by Stephen T. Davis. New York: St. Martin's Press, 1997, 98-101.

Coakley, Sarah. "Does Kenosis Rest on a Mistake? Three Kenotic Models in Patristic Exegesis." In *Exploring Kenotic Christology: The Self-Emptying of God,* edited by C. Stephen Evans. Oxford: Oxford University Press, 2006, 246–64.

———. "Is the Resurrection an 'Historical' Event? Some Muddles and Mysteries." In *The Resurrection of Jesus Christ,* edited by Paul D. L. Avis. London: D.L.T., 1993, 85–115.

————. "*Kenosis*: Theological Meanings and Gender Connotations." In *The Work of Love: Creation as Kenosis,* edited by John Polkinghorne. Grand Rapids, MI: Eerdmans, 2001, 192–210.

————. "The Resurrection: The Grammar of 'Raised.'" In *Biblical Concepts and Our World,* edited by D. Z. Phillips and Mario von der Ruhr. Basingstoke: Palgrave, 2004, 169–189.

Cross, Richard. "Atonement Without Satisfaction." In *Oxford Readings in Philosophical Theology, Vol. 1, Trinity, Incarnation, and Atonement,* edited by Michael C. Rea. Oxford: Oxford University Press, 2009, 328-347.

————. "The Incarnation." In *The Oxford Handbook of Philosophical Theology,* edited by Thomas P. Flint and Michael C. Rea. Oxford: Oxford University Press, 2009, 452-475.

Evans, Stephen C. "The Incarnational Narrative as Myth and History." *The Christian Scholars Review* 23, no. 4 (June, 1994), 387-407.

Graham, Gordon. "Atonement." In *The Cambridge Companion to Christian Philosophical Theology,* edited by Charles Taliaferro and Chad V. Meister. Cambridge: Cambridge University Press, 2010, 124-135.

Hick, John. "Is the Doctrine of the Atonement a Mistake?" In *Reason and the Christian Religion: Essays in Honour of Richard Swinburne,* edited by Alan G. Padgett. Oxford: Clarendon Press, 1994, 247-264.

Lewis, David. "Do we Believe in Penal Substitution?" In *Oxford Readings in Philosophical Theology: Vol. 1: Trinity, Incarnation, and Atonement*, edited by Michael C. Rea. Oxford: Oxford University Press, 2009308-314.

Lucas, J. R. "Atonement and Redemption." In *Freedom and Grace*, by J. R. Lucas. London: SPCK, 1976, 50-63.

————. "Reflections on the Atonement." In *Reason and the Christian Religion: Essays in Honour of Richard Swinburne*, edited by Alan G. Padgett. Oxford: Clarendon Press, 1994, 265-276.

Marshall, Bruce D. "Debt, Punishment, and Payment: A Meditation on the Cross, in Light of St. Anselm," *Nova et Vetera* (English Edition) volume 9, no. 1 (Winter 2011), 163-181.

Moser, Paul. "The Crisis of the Cross: God as Scandalous." In *Mel Gibson's Passion and Philosophy:The Cross, the Questions, the Controverssy*, edited by Jorge J. E. Garcia. La Salle, Ill.: Open Court, 2004, 204-217.

Porter, Steven L. "Swinburnian Atonement and the Doctrine of Penal Substitution." In *Oxford Readings in Philosophical Theology: Vol. 1: Trinity, Incarnation, and Atonement*, edited by Michael C. Rea. Oxford: Oxford University Press, 2009, 314-327.

Purtill, Richard L. "Justice, Mercy, Supererogation, and Atonement." In *Christian Philosophy*, edited by

Thomas P. Flint. Notre Dame: University of Notre Dame Press, 1990, 37-50.

Quinn, Philip L. "Abelard on Atonement: 'Nothing Unintelligible, Arbitrary, Illogical, or Immoral About It.'" In *Oxford Readings in Philosophical Theology: Vol. 1: Trinity, Incarnation, and Atonement*, edited by Michael C. Rea. Oxford: Oxford University Press, 2009, 348-364.

————. "Christian Atonement and Kantian Justification." *Faith and Philosophy* 3, no. 4 (1986) 440-462.

————. "Swinburne on Guilt, Atonement, and Christian Redemption." In *Reason and the Christian Religion: Essays in Honour of Richard Swinburne*, edited by Alan G. Padgett. Oxford: Clarendon Press, 1994, 277-299.

Soskice, Janet Martin. "Blood and Defilement." In *The Kindness of God: Metaphor, Gender, and Religious Language* by Janet Martin Soskice. Oxford: Oxford University Press, 2007, 84-99.

Stump, Eleonore. "Atonement According to Aquinas." In *Oxford Readings in Philosophical Theology: Vol. 1: Trinity, Incarnation, and Atonement*, edited by Michael C. Rea. Oxford: Oxford University Press, 2009, 267-293.

————. "Atonement and the Cry of Dereliction from the Cross." *European Journal for Philosophy of Religion* 4, no. 1 (Spring 2012), 1-17.

————. "The Nature of the Atonement." In *Reason, Metaphysics, and Mind: New Essays on the*

Philosophy of Alvin Plantinga, edited by Kelly Clark and Michael Rea. Oxford: Oxford University Press, 2012, 128-144.

Swinburne, Richard. *Responsibility and Atonement.* Oxford: Clarendon Press, 1989.

Tanner, Kathryn E. "Incarnation, Cross, and Sacrifice: A Feminist-Inspired Reappraisal" *Anglican Theological Review* vol. 86, no. 1 (Winter 2004) 35-56.

5

Pneumatology

Person and Work

Abraham, William J. "The Epistemological Significance of the Inner Witness of the Holy Spirit." In *Faith and Philosophy* 7, no. 4 (1990) 434-50.

Alston, William P. "The Holy Spirit and the Trinity." In *Philosophy and Theological Discourse*, edited by Stephen T. Davis. New York: St. Martin's Press, 1997, 102-123.

————. "The Indwelling of the Holy Spirit." In *Divine Nature and Human Language: Essays in Philosophical Theology,* by William P. Alston. Ithaca: Cornell University Press, 1989, 223-252.

Bouchard, Charles E. "Recovering the Gifts of the Holy Spirit in Moral Theology." *Theological Studies* 63, no. 3 (2002), 539-558.

Florensky, Pavel Aleksandrovich. "On the Holy Spirit." In *Ultimate Questions: An Anthology of Russian Religious Thought*, edited by Alexander Schmemann. New York: Holt, Reinhart and Winston, 1965, 137-172.

Marshall, Bruce D. "Action and Person: Do Palamas and Aquinas Agree about the Spirit?" *St. Vladimir's*

Theological Quarterly 39, no. 4 (1995), 379-408; also in *Der Heilige Geist: Ökumenische und reformatorische Untersuchungen*, Veröffentlichungen der Luther-Akademie Ratzeburg 25 (Erlangen: Martin-Luther-Verlag, 1996), 189-213.

———. "The Deep Things of God: Trinitarian Pneumatology." In *The Oxford Handbook of the Trinity*, edited by Gilles Emery and Matthew Levering. Oxford: Oxford University Press, 2011, 400-413.

———. "What Does the Spirit Have to Do?" In *Reading John With St. Thomas Aquinas*, edited by Michael Dauphinais and Matthew Levering. Washington, D.C.: Catholic University of America Press, 2005, 62-77.

Pinsent, Andrew. "The Gifts and Fruits of the Holy Spirit." In *The Oxford Handbook of Aquinas*, edited by Brian Davies and Eleonore Stump. Oxford: Oxford University Press, 2012, 475-490.

Price, H. H. "Paranormal Cognition, Symbolism, and Inspiration." In *Essays in the Philosophy of Religion*, by H. H. Price. Oxford: Clarendon Press, 1972.

Runzo, Joseph. "The Third Person of The Trinity." In *Philosophy and Theological Discourse*, edited by Stephen T. Davis. New York: St. Martin's Press, 1997, 124-129.

Tanner, Kathryn E. "Workings of the Spirit: Simplicity or Complexity?" In *The Work of the Spirit: Pneumatology and Pentecostalism*, edited by

Michael Welker. Grand Rapids, Mich: William B. Eerdmans Pub. Co, 2006, 87-108.

Wainwright, Geoffrey. "The Holy Spirit." In *The Cambridge Companion to Christian Doctrine,* edited by Colin E. Gunton. Cambridge: Cambridge University Press, 1997, 273-296

6

Ecclesiology

Nature, Word and Sacraments, Ministry, Purpose or Mission

Abraham, William J. "Church." In *The Cambridge Companion to Christian Philosophical Theology*, edited by Charles Taliaferro and Chad V. Meister. Cambridge: Cambridge University Press, 2010, 170-182.

———."Church and Churches: Ecumenism." In *The Oxford Handbook of Evangelical Theology*, edited by Gerald McDermott. New York: Oxford University Press, 2010, 296-309.

———. "Episcopacy, Athanasius, and the Politics of Church Renewal." Unpublished.

———. "Handing On the Teaching of the Apostles: Canonical Episcopacy." In *Canonical Theism*, edited by William J. Abraham, Jason E. Vickers, and Natalie B. Van. Grand Rapids, Mich.: Eerdmans, 2008, 43-60.

Coakley, Sarah. "'In Persona Christi': Gender, Priesthood and the Nuptial Metaphor." *Svensk Teologisk Kvartalskrift* 82 (2006), 145–54, a lecture delivered on the occasion of the receipt of the degree Theologiae Doctricem Honoris Causa, University of Lund.

―――. "Lay and Ordained Ministries: Some Theological Reflections." *Sewanee Theological Journal* 43 (2000), 207–213.

―――. "The Woman at the Altar: Cosmological Disturbance or Gender Fluidity?" *The Anglican Theological Review* 86 (2004), 75–93.

Del Colle, Ralph. "The Church." In *The Oxford Handbook of Systematic Theology,* edited by J. B. Webster, Kathryn Tanner, and Iain R. Torrance. Oxford: Oxford University Press, 2007, 249-266.

Dulles, Avery. *Models of the Church.* New York: Doubleday, 2002.

Dummett, Michael. "The Intelligibility of Eucharistic Doctrine." ." In *The Rationality of Religious Belief: Essays in Honour of Basil Mitchell,* edited by William J. Abraham and Steven W. Holtzer. Oxford: Oxford University Press, 1987, 231-262.

Fahey, Michael A. "Sacraments." In *The Oxford Handbook of Systematic Theology,* edited by J. B. Webster, Kathryn Tanner, and Iain R. Torrance. Oxford: Oxford University Press, 2007, 267-284.

Farrow, Douglas. "Church, Ecumenism, and Eschatology." In *The Oxford Handbook of Eschatology,* edited by Jerry L. Walls. Oxford: Oxford University Press, 2008, 347-364.

Griffiths, Paul J. "Christians and the Church." In *The Oxford Handbook of Theological Ethics,* edited by

Gilbert Meilaender and Bill Werpehowski. Oxford: Oxford University Press, 2005, 398-412.

Insole, Christopher J. "The Truth Behind Practices: Wittgenstein, Robinson Crusoe and Ecclesiology." *Studies in Christian Ethics*, 20 (2007), 364-382.

Jenson, Robert W. "The Church and the Sacraments." In *The Cambridge Companion to Christian Doctrine*, edited by Colin E. Gunton. Cambridge: Cambridge University Press, 1997, 207-225.

Khomiakov, Aleksei. "The Church is One." In *On Spiritual Unity: A Slavophile Reader*, edited by Boris Jakim and Robert Bird. Hudson, NY: Lindisfarne Books, 1998, 31-54.

Kirmmse, Bruce H. "The Thunderstorm: Kierkegaard's Ecclesiology." *Faith and Philosophy* 17 (2000), 87-102.

Lucas, J. R. "The Eucharist: A University Sermon." In *Freedom and Grace,* by J. R. Lucas. London: SPCK, 1976, 109-119.

Marshall, Bruce D. "The Church in the Gospel," *Pro Ecclesia* 1, no. 1 (1992), 27-41; a shorter version, with "Irreversibility" (reply to interpreters), in *Lutheran Forum* 27, no. 1 (1993), 24-30, 47.

———. "The Disunity of the Church and the Credibility of the Gospel," *Theology Today* 50, no. 1 (1993), 78-89.

———. "The Divided Church and its Theology," (review essay on Ephraim Radner, *The End of the Church*), *Modern Theology* 16, no. 3 (2000), 377-96.

———. "Do Christians Worship the God of Israel?" *Knowing the Triune God*, edited by James J. Buckley and David S. Yeago. Grand Rapids: Eerdmans, 2001, 231-264.

———. "Elder Brothers: John Paul II's Teaching on the Jewish People as a Question to the Church, " In *John Paul II and the Jewish People: A Christian-Jewish Dialogue*, edited by David Dahlin and Matthew Levering. Lanham, MD: Rowman and Littlefield, 2008, 113-129.

———. "The Jewish People and Christian Theology," In *The Cambridge Companion to Christian Doctrine*, edited by Colin E. Gunton. Cambridge: Cambridge University Press, 1997, 81-100.

———. "Judaism and Christianity," In *The Cambridge Dictionary of Christian Theology*, edited by Ian McFarland, David Fergusson, Karen Kilby and Iain Torrance. Cambridge: Cambridge University Press, 2011, 253a-255a.

———. "Lutherans, Bishops, and the Divided Church," *Ecclesiology* 1, no. 2 (2005), 25-42.

———. "*Quasi in Figura*: A Brief Reflection on Jewish Election, after Thomas Aquinas" and "Postscript and Prospect" (reply to Emmanuel Perrier and Trent Pomplun), *Nova et Vetera* (English Edition) 7, no. 2 (2009), 477-84, 523-8.

_____. "The Whole Mystery of Our Salvation: St. Thomas on the Eucharist as Sacrifice." In *Sacraments in Aquinas*, edited by Michael

Dauphinais and Matthew Levering. Chicago: Hillenbrand Books, 2009, 39-64.

Min, Anselm Kyongsuk. "Towards a Church both Visible and Catholic." In *Philosophy and Theological Discourse*, edited by Stephen T. Davis. New York: St. Martin's Press, 1997, 41-46.

Morerod, Charles. "The Trinity, the Church, and the Sacraments." In *The Oxford Handbook of the Trinity*, edited by Gilles Emery and Matthew Levering. Oxford: Oxford University Press, 2011, 428-441.

Pruss, Alexander. "The Eucharist: Real Presence of Real Absence." In *The Oxford Handbook of Philosophical Theology*, edited by Thomas P. Flint and Michael C. Rea. Oxford: Oxford University Press, 2009, 512-540.

Quinn, Philip L. "Kantian Philosophical Ecclesiology." In *Essays in Philosophy of Religion,* edited by Philip L. Quinn and Christian Miller. Oxford: Oxford University Press, 2006, 255-78.

Shakespeare, Steven. "Ecclesiology and Philosophy." In *The Routledge Companion to the Christian Church*, edited by Gerard Mannion and Lewis S. Mudge. London: Routledge, 2008, 655-673.

Taliaferro, Charles. "Religious Rites." In *The Cambridge Companion to Christian Philosophical Theology,* edited by Charles Taliaferro and Chad V. Meister. Cambridge: Cambridge University Press, 2010, 183-200.

Verheyden, Jack. "The Invisibility of the Church in American Protestant Theology and the Issue of

Catholic Reality." In *Philosophy and Theological Discourse*, edited by Stephen T. Davis. New York: St. Martin's Press, 1997, 22-40.

Wainwright, Geoffrey. "The Trinity in Liturgy and Preaching." In *The Oxford Handbook of the Trinity*, edited by Gilles Emery and Matthew Levering. Oxford: Oxford University Press, 2011, 457-471.

Zizioulas, Jean. *Being As Communion: Studies in Personhood and the Church*. Crestwood, N.Y.: St. Vladimir's Seminary Press, 1993.

7

Soteriology

*The Christian Life, Grace, Justification, Forgiveness,
Sanctification*

Abraham, William J. "The Epistemology of Conversion:
Is there something New?" In *Conversion in the
Wesleyan Tradition,* edited by Kenneth Collins and
John H. Tyson. Nashville: Abingdon, 2001, 175-194.
————. "Faith, Assurance, and Conviction: An
Epistemological Commentary on Hebrews 11:1." In
Ex Auditu 19, 2003, 65-75
————. "Grace and Freedom." In *An Introduction to the
Philosophy of Religion,* by William J. Abraham.
Englewood Cliffs: Prentice Hall, 1985, 142-151.
————. "Loyal Opposition and the Epistemology of
Conscience." In *Asbury Theological Journal* 56
(2001), 135-147.
Adams, Robert. "Pure Love." In *The Virtue of Faith and
Other Essays in Philosophical Theology,* by Robert
Adams. New York: Oxford University Press, 1987,
174-192.

———. "Saints." In *The Virtue of Faith and Other Essays in Philosophical Theology,* by Robert Adams. New York: Oxford University Press, 1987, 164-173.

———. "The Virtue of Faith." In *The Virtue of Faith and Other Essays in Philosophical Theology,* by Robert Adams. New York: Oxford University Press, 1987, 9-24.

Coakley, Sarah. "Charismatic Experience: Praying 'In the Spirit.'" In *We Believe in the Holy Spirit,* Doctrine Commission of the Church of England. London: Church House Publishing, 1991, 17–36

———."Dark Contemplation and Epistemic Transformation: The Analytic Philosopher Re-meets Teresa of Avila." In *Analytic Theology: New Essays in the Philosophy of Theology,* edited by Oliver D. Crisp and Michael C. Rea. Oxford: Oxford University Press, 2009, 280-312.

———. "On the Fearfulness of Forgiveness: Psalm 130:4 and its Theological Implications." In *Meditations of the Heart: The Psalms in Early Christian Thought and Practice,* edited by Andreas Andreopoulos, Augustine Casiday and Carol Harrison. Turnhout: Brepols, 2011, 33–51.

DeVries, Dawn. "Justification." In *The Oxford Handbook of Systematic Theology,* edited by J. B. Webster, Kathryn Tanner, and Iain R. Torrance. Oxford: Oxford University Press, 2007, 197-211.

Evans, Stephen C. "Catholic-Protestant Views of Justification: How Should Christians View Theological Disagreements?" In *The Redemption: An*

Interdisciplinary Symposium on Christ asRedeemer, edited by Stephen T. Davis, Daniel Kendall, and Gerald O'Collins. Oxford:Oxford University Press, 2004, 255-273.

————. "Salvation, Sin, and Human Freedom: A Kierkegaardian View." In *The Grace of God, The Will of Man*, edited by Clark Pinnock. Grand Rapids, Michigan: Zondervan, 1989, 181-189.

Fiddes, Paul. "Salvation." In *The Oxford Handbook of Systematic Theology*, edited by J. B. Webster, Kathryn Tanner, and Iain R. Torrance. Oxford: Oxford University Press, 2007, 176-196.

Frances, Bryan. "Spirituality, Expertise, and Philosophers." In *Oxford Studies in Philosophy of Religion: Vol. 1*, edited by Jonathan L. Kvanvig. Oxford: Oxford University Press 2008, 44-81.

Hare, John E. "Atonement, Justification, and Sanctification." In *A Companion to Philosophy of Religion*, edited by Philip L. Quinn and Charles Taliaferro. Cambridge, Mass: Blackwell, 1999, 549-555.

————. "Forgiveness, Justification, and Reconciliation." In *The Wisdom of the Christian Faith*, edited by Paul Moser and Michael McFall. Cambridge: Cambridge University Press, 2012, 77-98.

Hutter, Reinhard. "The Christian Life." In *The Oxford Handbook of Systematic Theology*, edited by J. B. Webster, Kathryn Tanner, and Iain R. Torrance. Oxford: Oxford University Press, 2007, 285-305.

Jantzen, Grace M. "Conspicuous Sanctity and Religious Belief." In *The Rationality of Religious Belief: Essays in Honour of Basil Mitchell*, edited by William J. Abraham and Steven W. Holtzer. Oxford: Oxford University Press, 1987, 121-140.

Keating, Daniel A. "Trinity and Salvation: Christian Life as an Existence in the Trinity." In *The Oxford Handbook of the Trinity*, edited by Gilles Emery and Matthew Levering. Oxford: Oxford University Press, 2011, 442-456.

Lucas, J.R. "Forgiveness." In *Freedom and Grace,* by J. R. Lucas. London: SPCK, 1976, 78-84.

―――. "Forgiveness and Frustration." In *Freedom and Grace,* by J. R. Lucas. London: SPCK, 1976, 69-77.

―――. "Grace." In *Freedom and Grace,* by J. R. Lucas. London: SPCK, 1976, 22-26.

Marshall, Bruce D. "After Augsburg: The Ecumenical Future of Justification," *International Journal for the Study of the Christian Church* 2, no. 1 (2002), 21-37.

―――. "The Argument is Over" (on the Lutheran/Roman Catholic Joint Declaration on Justification). *The Tablet* 255 (April 7, 2001).

―――. "*Beatus vir*: Thomas d'Aquin, Romains 4, et le role de l'imputation dans la justification," *Revue thomiste* 111, no. 1 (2011), 3-34; shorter English version, "*Beatus vir*: Aquinas, Romans 4, and the Role of 'Reckoning' in Justification," *Reading Romans with St. Thomas Aquinas: Ecumenical Explorations*, edited by Matthew Levering and

Michael Dauphinais. Washington, D.C., Catholic University of America Press, 2012.

————. "Justification as Declaration and Deification," *International Journal of Systematic Theology* 4, no. 1 (2002), 3-28.

————. "Justification 2: Historical and Systematic Theology," *The Encyclopedia of Christianity*, edited by E. Fahlbusch, J. M. Lochman, J. Mbiti, J. Pelikan, & L. Vischer, vol. 3. Grand Rapids: Eerdmans & Leiden: Brill, 2003, 93-100.

McFarland, Ian A. "Nature, Grace, and Agency." *Theology Today* 68 (2011), 324-330.

Moser, Paul K. "Faith." In *Being Good: Christian Virtues for Everyday Life, edited by* Michael K Austin and Douglas Geivett. Grand Rapids: Eerdmans, 2011, 13-29.

————. "Sin and Salvation." In *The Cambridge Companion to Christian Philosophical Theology,* edited by Charles Taliaferro and Chad V. Meister. Cambridge: Cambridge University Press, 2010, 136-151.

Mitchell, Basil. "The Grace of God." In *Faith and Logic: Oxford Essays in Philosophical Theology* edited by Basil Mitchell. London: Allen & Unwin, 1958, 149-175.

Moser, Paul K. "Faith." In *Being Good: Christian Virtues for Everyday Life*, edited by Michael Austin and Douglas Geivett. Grand Rapids: Eerdmans, 2012, 13-29.

————. "God, Flux, and the Agape Struggle." Forthcoming in *Oxford Studies in Philosophy of Religion*, Vol. IV (2012).

O'Neill, Onora. "The Power of Example." *Philosophy*, 61 (1986), 5-29.

Plantinga, Alvin. "Supralapsarianism, or 'O Felix Culpa.'" In *Christian Faith and the Problem of Evil*, edited by Peter Van Inwagen. Grand Rapids: William B. Eerdmans Publishing Co, 2004, 1-25.

Pojman, Louis P. "In Defense of Moral Saints." *Ethical Theory: Classical and Contemporary Readings*, by Louis P. Pojman. Belmont, Cal.: Wadsworth, 1989.

Sherry, Patrick. "Philosophy and the Saints." *Heythrop Journal* (January 1977).

————. *Saints, Spirituality, and Immortality*. Albany: State University of New York Press, 1984.

————. "What is Redemption?" In *Images of Redemption*, by Patrick Sherry. London: T&T Clark, 2003, 22-48.

Stump, Eleonore. "Atonement and Justification." In *Trinity, Incarnation, and Atonement: Philosophical and Theological Essays*, edited, Ronald Jay Feenstra and Cornelius Plantinga. Notre Dame: University of Notre Dame Press, 1989, 178-209.

————. "Grace and Free Will." In *Le don et la dette*, edited by Marco Olivetti, (Biblioteca Dell' Archivio Di Filosofia, Casa Editrice Dott. Antonio Milani, CEDAM, 2004), 411-418.

————. "Justifying Faith, Free Will, and the Atonement." In *Freedom and the Human Person*

(Studies in Philosophy and the History of Philosophy), edited by Richard Velkley. Washington, D. C.: Catholic University of America Press, 2007, 90-105.

———. "Sancification, Hardening of the Heart, and Frankfurt's Concept of Free Will." *The Journal of Philosophy* 85 (1982), 395-420.

Swinburne, Richard. "The Christian Scheme of Salvation." In *Oxford Readings in Philosophical Theology: Vol. 1: Trinity, Incarnation, and Atonement*, edited by Michael C. Rea. Oxford: Oxford University Press, 2009, 294-307.

Tanner, Kathryn E. "Creation and Salvation in the Image of an Incomprehensible God." In *God of Salvation: Soteriology in Theological Perspective,* edited by Ivor J. Davidson and Murray Rae. Farnham, Surrey, England: Ashgate, 2011, 61-76.

———. "The End of Nature and the Last Human?: Thinking Theologically about 'Nature' in a Postnatural Condition." In *Without Nature? :a New Condition for Theology*, edited by David Albertson and Cabell King. New York: Fordham University Press, 2010, 363-376

———. "Justification and Justice in a Theology of Grace" *Theology Today* vol. 55, no. 4 (January 1999), 510-523.

Urmson, J. O. "Saints and Heroes." In *Essays in Moral Philosophy*, edited by A. I. Melden. Seattle: University of Washington Press, 1958, 198-216.

Walsh, Sylvia. "Moral Character and Temptation." In *The*

Wisdom of the Christian Faith, edited by Paul Moser and Michael McFall, 121–37. Cambridge: Cambridge University Press, 2012.

Westphal, Merold. "Hermeneutics and Holiness." In *Analytic Theology: New Essays in the Philosophy of Theology*, edited by Oliver D. Crisp and Michael C. Rea. Oxford: Oxford University Press, 2009, 265-280.

———. "Repentance and Self-Knowledge." In *The Wisdom of the Christian Faith*, edited by Paul Moser and Michael McFall. Cambridge: Cambridge University Press, 2012, 39–57.

Wolf, Susan. "Moral Saints." *The Journal of Philosophy* LXXIX (1982), 419-439.

Wolterstorff, Nicholas. "Does Forgiveness Undermine Justice?" In *God and the Ethics of Belief, New Essays in Philosophy of Religion,* edited by Andrew Cole and Andrew Chignell. Cambridge: Cambridge University Press, 2005, 219-247.

8

Eschatology

The Last Things, Death and eternal life (personal eschatology: death, the intermediate state, heaven, hell, and ultimate destiny), (cosmic eschatology: parousia or return of Christ, the final destiny of all things)

Abraham, William J. "Eschatology and Epistemology." In *The Oxford Handbook of Eschatology*, edited by Jerry L. Walls. Oxford: Oxford University Press, 2008, 581-595.

———. "Life after Death." In *An Introduction to the Philosophy of Religion,* by William J. Abraham. Englewood Cliffs: Prentice Hall, 1985, 201-214.

Adams. Marilyn McCord. "Hell and the God of Justice." *Religious Studies* 11 (1975), 433-447.

Baker, Lynne Rudder. "Death and the Afterlife." In *The Oxford Handbook of Philosophy of Religion*, edited by William J. Wainwright. New York: Oxford University Press, 2005, 366-391.

Bauckham, Richard. "Eschatology." In *The Oxford Handbook of Systematic Theology,* edited by J. B. Webster, Kathryn Tanner, and Iain R. Torrance. Oxford: Oxford University Press, 2007, 306-324.

Brown, Christopher. "Friendship in Heaven: Aquinas on Supremely Perfect Happiness and the Communion of the Saints." In *Metaphysics and God: Essays in Honor of Eleonore Stump*, edited by Kevin Timpe. New York: Routledge, 2009, 225-248.

Craig, William Lane. "Time, Eternity, and Eschatology." In *The Oxford Handbook of Eschatology*, edited by Jerry L. Walls. Oxford: Oxford University Press, 2008, 596-613.

Davis, Stephen T. "Eschatology and Resurrection." In *The Oxford Handbook of Eschatology*, edited by Jerry L. Walls. Oxford: Oxford University Press, 2008, 384-398.

———. "Survival of Death." In *A Companion to Philosophy of Religion*, edited by Philip L. Quinn and Charles Taliaferro. Cambridge, Mass: Blackwell, 1999, 556-561.

Daley, Brian. "Eschatology in the Early Church." In *The Oxford Handbook of Eschatology*, edited by Jerry L. Walls. Oxford: Oxford University Press, 2008, 91-112.

Eberl, Jason T. "Do Human Beings Persist between Death and Resurrection." In *Metaphysics and God: Essays in Honor of Eleonore Stump*, edited by Kevin Timpe. New York: Routledge, 2009, 188-205.

Farrow, Douglas. "Resurrection and Immortality." In *The Oxford Handbook of Systematic Theology*, edited by J. B. Webster, Kathryn Tanner, and Iain R. Torrance. Oxford: Oxford University Press, 2007, 212-235.

Ferguson, David. "Eschatology." In *The Cambridge Companion to Christian Doctrine,* edited by Colin E. Gunton. Cambridge: Cambridge University Press, 1997, 226-244.

Forrest, Peter. "The Tree of Life: Agency and Immortality in a Metaphysics Inspired by Quantum Theory." In *Persons: Human and Divine,* edited by Peter Van Inwagen and Dean W. Zimmerman. Oxford: Clarendon, 2007, 301-318.

Griffiths, Paul J. "Gaudium et Spes, Luctus et Angor: The Dramatic Character of the Human Condition." *Nova et Vetera* (English edition), 8, no. 2 (2010), 269-281.

———. "Is There a Doctrine of the Descent Into Hell?" *Pro Ecclesia* 17, no. 3 (2008), 257-268.

———. "Purgatory." In *The Oxford Handbook of Eschatology,* edited by Jerry L. Walls. Oxford: Oxford University Press, 2008, 427-446.

———. "Self-Annihilation: A Disputable Question in Christian Eschatology." *Pro Ecclesia* 16, no. 4 (2007), 416-444.

———. "Self-Annihilation or Damnation? A Disputable Question in Christian Eschatology." In *Liberal Faith: Essays in Honor of Philip Quinn,* edited by Paul J. Weithman. Notre Dame, Indiana: University of Notre Dame Press, 2008, 83-117.

Hart, David Bentley. "Death, Final Judgement, and the Meaning of Life." In *The Oxford Handbook of Eschatology,* edited by Jerry L. Walls. Oxford: Oxford University Press, 2008, 476-492.

Rombs, Ronnie J. *Saint Augustine & the Fall of the Soul: Beyond O'Connell & His Critics*. Washington, D.C.: Catholic University of America Press, 2006.

Kvanvig, Jonathan L. *The Problem of Hell*. New York: Oxford University Press, 1993.

Kvanvig, Jonathan L. "Heaven and Hell." In *A Companion to Philosophy of Religion*, edited by Philip L. Quinn and Charles Taliaferro. Cambridge, Mass: Blackwell, 1999, 562-569.

————. "Hell" In *The Oxford Handbook of Eschatology*, edited by Jerry L. Walls. Oxford: Oxford University Press, 2008, 413-426.

Merricks, Trenton. "The Resurrection of the Body and the Life Everlasting." In Michael J. Murray, ed. *Reason for the Hope Within*. Grand Rapids: Eerdmans, 1999, 261-286.

————. "The Resurrection of the Body." In *The Oxford Handbook of Philosophical Theology*, edited by Thomas P. Flint and Michael C. Rea. Oxford: Oxford University Press, 2009, 476-490.

Moser, Paul K. "Divine Hiddenness, Death, and Meaning." in *Philosophy of Religion: Classic and Contemporary Issues*, edited by P. Copan and C. Meister. Oxford: Blackwell, 2008, 215-27. Reprinted in *The Philosophy of Religion Reader*, edited by C. Meister. London: Routledge, 2008, 613-24, and in *Exploring the Meaning of Life*, edited by J. Seachris. Oxford: Wiley Blackwell, 2013, 481-91.

Murray, Michael J. "Heaven and Hell." In *Reason for the Hope Within*, edited by Michael J. Murray. Grand Rapids: Eerdmans, 1999, 287-317.

Pinnock, Clark H. "Annihilationism." In *The Oxford Handbook of Eschatology*, edited by Jerry L. Walls. Oxford: Oxford University Press, 2008, 462-476.

Price, H. H. "Two Conception of the Next World." In *Essays in the Philosophy of Religion: Based on the Sarum Lectures, 1971* by H. H. Price. Oxford: Clarendon Press, 1972.

————. "Motives for Disbelief in Life after Death." In *Essays in the Philosophy of Religion: Based on the Sarum Lectures, 1971* by H. H. Price. Oxford: Clarendon Press, 1972.

Ragland C. P. "Love and Damnation." In *Metaphysics and God: Essays in Honor of Eleonore Stump*, edited by Kevin Timpe. New York: Routledge, 2009, 206-224.

Rowland, Christopher. "The Eschatology of the New Testament." In *The Oxford Handbook of Eschatology*, edited by Jerry L. Walls. Oxford: Oxford University Press, 2008, 56-72.

Russell, Robert. "Cosmology and Eschatology." In *The Oxford Handbook of Eschatology*, edited by Jerry L. Walls. Oxford: Oxford University Press, 2008, 563-580.

Soskice, Janet Martin. "Being Lovely: Eschatological Anthropology." In *The Kindness of God: Metaphor, Gender, and Religious Language* by Janet Martin

Soskice. Oxford: Oxford University Press, 2007, 181-188.

Stump, Eleonore. "Resurrection and the Separated Soul." In *The Oxford Handbook of Aquinas*, edited by Brian Davies and Eleonore Stump. Oxford: Oxford University Press, 2012, 458-466.

————. "Resurrection, Reassembly, and Reconstitution: Aquinas on the Soul." In *Die menschliche Seele: Brauchen wir den Dualismus?*, edited by Bruno Niederberger and Edmund Runggaldier. Frankfurt: Ontos Verlag, 2006, 153-174.

Swinburne, Richard. "A Theodicy of Heaven and Hell." In *The Existence and Nature of God*, edited by Alfred J. Freddoso. Notre Dame: University of Notre Dame Press, 1983.

Talbot, Thomas. "The Doctrine of Everlasting Punishment." *Faith and Philosophy* 7 (1990), 19-42.

————. "Universalism." In *The Oxford Handbook of Eschatology*, edited by Jerry L. Walls. Oxford: Oxford University Press, 2008, 446-461.

Tanner, Kathryn E. "Eschatology Without a Future?" in *The End of the World and the Ends of God: Science and Theology on Eschatology*, edited by J. C. Polkinghorne and Michael Welker. Harrisburg, Pa: Trinity Press International, 2000, 222-237.

Van Inwagen, Peter. "The Possibility of Resurrection." In *The Possibility of Resurrection and Other Essays in Christian Apologetics,* by Peter Van Inwagen. Boulder: Westview, 1998, 45-52.

Walls, Jerry L. "Heaven and Hell." In *The Cambridge Companion to Christian Philosophical Theology*, edited by Charles Taliaferro and Chad V. Meister. Cambridge: Cambridge University Press, 2010, 238-252.

Weber, Timothy P. "Millennialism." In *The Oxford Handbook of Eschatology*, edited by Jerry L. Walls. Oxford: Oxford University Press, 2008, 365-383.

Walls, Jerry. "Heaven." In *The Oxford Handbook of Eschatology*, edited by Jerry L. Walls. Oxford: Oxford University Press, 2008, 399-412.

———. "Heaven and Hell." In *The Oxford Handbook of Philosophical Theology*, edited by Thomas P. Flint and Michael C. Rea. Oxford: Oxford University Press, 2009, 491-512.

———. *Heaven: The Logic of Eternal Joy*. Oxford: Oxford University Press, 2002.

———. *Hell: The Logic of Damnation*. Notre Dame: University of Notre Dame Press, 1992.

———. "The Wisdom of Hope in a Despairing World." In *The Wisdom of the Christian Faith*, edited by Paul Moser and Michael McFall. Cambridge: Cambridge University Press, 2012, 244–64.

Van Lommel, P. *et al.* "Near-death experience in survivors of cardiac arrest: a prospective study in the Netherlands." *Lancet* 2001, 358: 2039-2045.

Zaleski, Carol. "Near-Death Experiences." In *The Oxford Handbook of Eschatology*, edited by Jerry L. Walls. Oxford: Oxford University Press, 2008, 614-629.

————. *The Life of the World To Come*. New York: Oxford University Press, 1996.

About the Author

Born in Northern Ireland in 1947, William J. Abraham currently teaches at Perkins School of Theology, Southern Methodist University in Dallas, Texas. Educated at Portora Royal School, Enniskillen and Queen's University, Belfast, Abraham went on to receive a Master of Divinity Degree from Asbury Theological Seminary in Wilmore, Kentucky, and a doctorate in Philosophy of Religion from the University of Oxford, England. In 2008 he was awarded the D.D (h.c.) from Asbury Theological Seminary.

Other books written or edited by Professor Abraham that relate to the theme of this book include *An Introduction to the Philosophy of Religion* (Englewood Cliffs: Prentice Hall, 1985), *The Divine Inspiration of Holy Scripture* (Oxford: Oxford University Press, 1981); *Divine Revelation and the Limits of Historical Criticism* (Oxford: Oxford University Press, 1982); *The Logic of Evangelism* (Grand Rapids: Eerdmans, 1989). *Canon and Criterion in Christian Theology: From the Fathers to Feminism* (Oxford: Clarendon Press, 1998); *The Logic of Renewal* (Grand Rapids: Eerdmans, 2003), *Canonical Theism: A Proposal for Theology and the Church* (Grand Rapids: Eerdmans, 2008), and *Crossing the Threshold of Divine Revelation* (Grand Rapids, Mich: Eerdmans Pub, 2006).